all that
glitters

all that
glitters

pearl lowe

HODDER

First published in Great Britain in 2007 by Hodder & Stoughton
A division of Hodder Headline
First published in paperback in 2008

A Hodder & Stoughton Book

3

A CIP catalogue record for this title is available from the British Library

ISBN 978 0 340 93320 6

Typeset in Bembo by Hewer Text UK Ltd, Edinburgh

Printed and bound by CPI Mackays, Chatham, ME5 8TD

Hodder Headline's policy is to use papers that are natural, renewable
and recyclable products and made from wood grown in sustainable forests.
The logging and manufacturing processes are expected to conform
to the environmental regulations of the country of origin.

Hodder & Stoughton Ltd
A division of Hodder Headline
338 Euston Road
London NW1 3BH

Picture acknowledgements
Most of the photos are from the author's collection.

Additional sources:
Section 1, page 1: Russ Allen Ltd; page 6 centre: courtesy Melody Maker/NME;
6 below: courtesy NME; 8 below: Lili Wilde/Parkway.
Section 2: page 1: Justin Edward John Smith; page 5 and 6 below: Luke Kirwan; 6 above:
Phil Knott; 7 centre & below, 8 below left & below right: Getty Images.

Every reasonable effort has been made to contact the copyright holders, but if
there are any errors or omissions, Hodder & Stoughton will be pleased to insert the
appropriate acknowledgement in any subsequent printing of this publication.

This book is for Mum, Dad, Danny, Daisy, Alfie, Frankie, Betty and Zoë. Without you, I wouldn't be here.

Through aches and pains,
that made us shiver,
we made our plans to stay together.
Through reddened eyes,
we spoke of child,
then came to realise,
it's not so wild, to feel no love,
only shame, when baby faces take all the blame.

Pearl Lowe and Danny Goffey 2000

ACKNOWLEDGEMENTS

Thank you to everyone for all your help and support.

In strict alphabetical order, mostly (!): Jessica Albarn, Annalisa Astarita, Carl Barat, Darren Berry, Andy Boyd, Sam Brick, Jeanette Calliva, Will Cameron, Alison Charles, Emma Comelly, Gaz Coombes, Rob Coombes, All at Courtyard, Helen Coyle, All at Crisis, All at The Cross, Patsy Daniel, Adam Davis, Cheryl Davis, Elaine Davis, Nick Davis, Mia Dolan, Nik Done, Mark Dempsey, Louis Elliot, Suzanna Flynn, Louise Gannon, Linda and Chris Goffey, Nick Goffey, Ed and Gita Harcourt, Jason Hetherington, All at Hodder, Suzanne Howlett, Parelle Hulme, Gemma Hunt, Rhys Ifans, Carol Ireland, Charles Jarvis, Emma Knight, Sara Lanchlan, Sarah Leon, All at Liberty, Pat Lomax, Lisa M, John McKeown, Asmat Mohanial, Claire Jardine Patterson, Jools Poore, All at Premier, Mick Quinn, Sarah Reygate, Lucie Richards, Marlon Richards, Jess Robertson, Adam Rutherford, Richard Scorer, All at Select, Emma Summerton, Emily Swan, Charlotte Taitte, Liv Tyler, All at Unity, Rowena Webb, Ellen Wigan, Murphy Williams.

And a huge thank you to Natasha Garnett for everything, especially for being so patient and understanding and for being such a wonderful friend.

CONTENTS

I

Paris

It should have been a weekend to remember, but the truth is that my recollections of what actually happened over those three days in Paris in 1999 remain quite hazy. All I do know is that I ruined it for everyone. Through my own stupidity and selfishness, my own thoughtless actions, I let everyone down – my boyfriend Danny Goffey, who I had come to Paris to see perform with his band Supergrass, during the French leg of their European tour; and my best friend Zoë Grace, whose birthday we were supposed to be celebrating in the City of Lights that weekend. But, most of all, I let myself down, by behaving like the shameless drug addict I had become.

And now I am sitting on a bench at the Gare du Nord station, waiting for the train that's going to take me back to London. My head pounds, my hands are shaking, my limbs ache and I am overwhelmed by waves of nausea. Even though it is a warm and sunny day outside, I am so cold that Danny has to wrap me in his jacket. He holds me close but says nothing. There is no point: he said it all this morning when I woke up, trembling, in my hotel bed. The train arrives, and with his help I manage to make it into our carriage. I slump into my seat, and lay my heavy head against the window. I try to speak but I'm finding it quite hard. All I can manage is a whisper. 'I'm sorry, I'm so sorry,' I say again and again.

I am filled with shame, remorse and anger. I wish I didn't have to make this journey. I wish that I could be at home right now in my bed in our house in Camden. I wish that I could turn back the clock. I wish that none of this had happened. And as these thoughts come to me, and flashes of what happened the night before start to haunt me, I begin to think I wish I was dead.

The irony of all this is that I had been really looking forward to my trip to Paris and had been planning it for weeks. Since Danny had left to go on tour with the band a couple of months before, I had felt quite lost without him and couldn't wait to see him again. In the four years since we first got together I had grown used to the fact there were periods of time when we had to be apart – that's what happened when you were going out with someone in the music industry. There would be promotional trips abroad, nights away when he was performing at gigs and festivals, weeks apart when he was on tour. Having worked for many years in the industry myself as the lead singer of a band, I understood that world. I knew that if our relationship was to survive then I would have to cope with those absences, and for the most part I did. But this time it was different, things were different, and I was finding it very hard to cope without him.

I was 31 now and had three children – the youngest, Frankie, born just four months earlier. I was no longer in a position where I could follow Danny round the country, or indeed the world, for long stretches of time. My place was at home with my ten-year-old daughter Daisy, our son Alfie, who was about to celebrate his third birthday, and my baby son. And so when Danny suggested that I meet him in Paris that weekend I couldn't have been happier. Although I was loath to leave the children behind, I knew that this short break was what I needed. My mother agreed. Sensing the strain I had been under in the last few months, she encouraged me to go, and offered to look after the children with the help of our nanny whilst I was gone. And so I started to plan my trip.

I would arrive on Thursday afternoon, having taken the Eurostar from Waterloo to Paris. After checking into the luxurious hotel room that had been booked for us by the tour promoters, I would wait for Danny to return from his rehearsals and we would then stroll out into the city. We would spend a couple of hours sightseeing before heading off for a romantic dinner on our own. On Friday we would go shopping, and when Danny left for his sound-check after lunch I would meet up with Zoë, my oldest and closest friend. She was coming to Paris to celebrate her birthday, and we planned to have a couple of drinks together at the hotel bar before we headed off to the Supergrass gig that evening. The rest of the weekend would be spent relaxing in bed, enjoying leisurely breakfasts and lunches and catching up.

By the time Thursday came, everything was in place. My bags were packed, my passport and ticket were at hand, and I had presented my mother with a long list of instructions for the children. There was just one more thing I needed to do before I left for Paris, and that was to make a call.

He was there within the hour, just as he said he would be, just as he always was. He knocked at the door and I let him into the hallway of our house. After exchanging a few pleasantries we got down to business. As I fumbled in my handbag for my wallet and the wad of crisp £20 notes I had taken from the cash machine the night before, he reached into his pocket and in return gave me what I had requested when we had spoken that morning. It was a small cellophane bag, no bigger than the palm of my hand, and it contained four grams of heroin – a gram for every day that I would be away. I always liked to be prepared.

Most people would think twice about carrying four grams of an illegal Class A drug from one country to another, but as I arrived at Waterloo I wasn't worried. My primary concern was that I had scored, and that was all that mattered to me at that moment in time. Knowing that the contents of my handbag would be checked at security, I had the foresight to stash my bag of drugs in the inside pocket of my coat, reassuring myself that it was highly unlikely that I, a smartly dressed mother of three, would be hauled aside for a strip search, and as I took my seat on the train I couldn't help feeling slightly smug about the fact that I had got away with it. It wasn't until I reached the Gare du Nord that the gravity of what I was doing hit me. As I got off the train I saw that there were sniffer dogs everywhere. I started to panic, not knowing what to do next. Should I go back on to the train and dump the bag under a seat? Should I surreptitiously drop it on the platform floor, hoping that no one would see? What a waste that would be. In the end I did neither: the dogs weren't interested in me or what I was carrying, and I walked past them without incident.

Having checked into our hotel room I pulled off my coat and opened the bedroom windows. I looked out on to Paris, and as I took in my surroundings I couldn't really believe that

I was there, it all seemed such a world away from Camden. Seeing the time, I realised that Danny wouldn't be back for at least an hour. Having unpacked, hung up my clothes, checked out the bathroom and flicked through the television channels, I sat on the bed wondering what to do next. I picked up my coat from the chair I had dropped it on and was about to hang it in the cupboard when I remembered what was in the pocket. I reached into it and there it was, my little bag, filled to the brim with that yellowy brown powder. Well, why not? I thought. I'm on holiday. A little smoke to celebrate, what's the harm in that?

I took out a small piece of foil from my bag and a lighter. Holding the foil between my finger and thumb, I placed a small pinch of powder in the centre of it and with my other hand I held the lighter and lit the foil from below. As the heroin heated, transforming itself from a sand-coloured powder to a tar-like liquid, I inhaled deeply. Just a couple of puffs, I told myself. A couple of puffs to get me going, then I will stop. I'll put it away and save it for later. I'll put it away and I'll stop. But, of course, being the addict that I was, I didn't put it away and I didn't stop.

When Danny arrived at the hotel it was late afternoon. I must have been smoking on and off for a couple of hours by this time and had gone through almost two grams of my supply. Danny wasn't amused. He wasn't angry with me for using – he was well aware of my habit by this stage – he was simply annoyed that I had taken so much of it. Like me, Danny enjoyed his drugs and was by no means immune to the odd fix of heroin, and the fact that I had managed to plough through most of the supply meant that there would be less for him.

But, unlike me, Danny always knew when to draw the line. A couple of hits could see him right, would give him the high he needed, and then he would stop. But for me it was different. I didn't have the boundaries that he had, or the will-power. My appetite for drugs was insatiable.

I think we both knew we weren't going anywhere that night. There would be no walks round the city, no sightseeing and no candle-lit dinners for us. Instead we would spend the night in, locked in our hotel room, lying on our bed, smoking heroin until the dawn broke.

In the morning, despite having not slept the night before, Danny and I decided that we should at least try to venture outside our hotel room. We were in Paris, after all. It was a beautiful day and at first the walk seemed to do me the world of good. After half an hour I decided that I wanted to go shopping, and so we headed to the Chloé Boutique on the Rue du Faubourg Saint-Honoré. I had been given a discount card to the store, and so this was to be our first port of call. The shop itself was beautiful, and the clothes were so exquisite I wanted them all. The shop assistant selected an array of dresses, trousers and tops for me to try on and ushered me into a changing-room. Undressed, I sat on a stool and pulled on a pair of Chloé jeans with a lion motif on the back pocket and a camisole top that I had had my eye on for some time. They fitted perfectly, but as I stood up to look at myself in the mirror I thought I was going to faint. Blood rushed from my head, and my knees buckled beneath me. With an outstretched arm I managed to steady myself against the wall and breathed in deeply.

'Everything OK, Madame?' came a voice from outside the cubicle.

'Fine, great,' I muttered.

I sat down and put my head between my legs for a moment, trying to catch my breath. Once my head stopped spinning I looked up and saw the hangers of clothes that had been put in the changing-room for me to try on. Blouses, jackets, a wonderful dress, a pair of tailored trousers . . . Beautiful as they all were, and much as I wanted them, just looking at them was making me feel claustrophobic. There is just no way I can do this, I thought. I have to get out of here. I have to go back to the hotel. Somehow I managed to muster enough strength to get back into my own clothes, and as I walked out of the changing-room I handed the assistant the jeans and the top. 'I'll just take these,' I said.

'Are you sure, Madame? What about the dress and the trousers? You didn't like them?'

'Oh, I liked them . . . they were lovely, but for now I'll just have these,' I said.

Danny looked at me. 'Are you OK?'

'Not really . . . I think I need to go back to the hotel. Now.'

By the time we got back to our room I was feeling so drained and weak I could barely stand. I was well aware of what was happening to me, and also of what I had to do to make myself feel better. I was withdrawing from heroin, and there was only one thing that would sort me out — and that was another fix. Danny was due to meet up with the rest of the band at the venue for a final rehearsal and a sound-check before the gig. Once he had made sure I was OK he headed off, and as the door closed behind him I reached into my handbag and pulled out my gear. To my horror there was hardly anything left in the bag — it was almost empty. I had gone through over three and a quarter grams in less than 24 hours. I began to panic. Now that I was starting to withdraw, I needed the drug not for kicks but just to make me feel normal. Without it I would become extremely ill; without it I would go through cold turkey. I looked at the remnants of the bag again. All that was left was a couple of smokes. It was not enough to see me through the rest of the trip – it wasn't even enough to get me through the night.

If I had been at home in London, this would have been the time that I would have made the call. I would have smoked what I had left to give me the lift I needed until one of my dealers came to my rescue. But I wasn't in London, I was in Paris, and although the drug was rife in France during that period, I didn't know how to get hold of it. I didn't know any dealers; I didn't even know anyone here who used it.

For a brief moment I considered saving what I had left until later on, until I really needed it, but as the symptoms of my withdrawal became more acute I abandoned the idea. I was starting to go through cold turkey. I desperately needed another fix. If I had been sensible I would, at this stage, have rung for a doctor and asked for some methadone. A prescribed and legal drug, methadone takes away the symptoms of withdrawal, without giving you the high of heroin. But I wasn't being sensible, I wasn't thinking straight. I didn't want methadone. I wanted smack and I was determined to get it. Something will turn up, I thought. Somehow I'll get some more. And so I opened the bag and reached for the foil and my lighter.

An hour or two must have passed when there was a knock at the door. I managed to get off the bed to answer it. It was Zoë, who was in high spirits. To get herself into the party mood Zoë and a friend had spent the best part of the journey from London to Paris sampling the delights of the Eurostar bar, and as she tumbled into the room she couldn't stop laughing. That was until she took one look at me.

It didn't take a rocket scientist to know what I had been up to. The stench in the room said it all. I had slumped back on to the bed in a daze, the pupils of my eyes dilated to the size of pinheads.

'Oh great!' she said. 'That's just bloody great! What a wonderful start to my birthday.'

At the time Zoë was one of the few people around me who knew of the extent of my drug taking. Although she liked a drink and a party, she was never into heroin, and my use of the drug had always upset her. She had tried to talk to me about it before, but she always knew that she was treading a fine line. Zoë was well aware that if she lectured me too much on the subject I would cut her out of my life altogether, just as I had with so many of my old friends by this stage. Looking at me now, lying on the bed curled up in the foetal position, nodding on and off, she knew that this wasn't the time for 'the talk'.

'What are we going to do with you?' she said, trying her best to sober up.

'I don't know . . .' I whined, burying my face into a pillow. 'I'm not feeling so great. I'm not sure I can face going out tonight.'

'But you have to! It's my birthday and I've come all this way to spend it with you.'

'I can't, Zoë, I just can't move.'

'Well, what about Danny? You can't miss his gig!'

'I just need another fix and I'll be fine.'

'Have you got any?'

'No.'

'Well, that's just great then.'

Eventually Zoë managed to talk me round, and at 8 p.m. we got into the minibus to take us to the venue. I was beginning to come down again and was starting to feel terrible. Every joint, every muscle in my body was beginning to ache, my head was throbbing and I had started to sweat, even though I was feeling cold. I just didn't know how I was going to make it through the night. When we arrived at the venue the band were on stage going through their final sound-check, so Zoë and I were ushered into their dressing-room by one of their French promoters. 'Make yourself at home,' he said. 'And if you want anything at all, just ask.'

By anything I suppose the promoter meant wine, champagne, something to eat even. But in my delirious state I decided to take what he said quite literally. As Zoë helped herself to a drink, I followed him out of the room.

'Excuse me,' I said.

'Yes?'

'I don't suppose . . . I don't suppose . . . you could get me some heroin?'

I mistook his look of surprise for one of misunderstanding.

'You know heroin? Smack? Could you get me some?'

He looked horrified. 'Non, non! I don't know about that, I don't know!' And with that he tutted loudly, turned his back on me and marched off.

There is a great double standard in the music industry when it comes to drugs. You see, had I asked almost any promoter in that world, for some cocaine, I would have had it there and then. They would either have given me a line from their own supply, or some lackey would have been sent out to buy it for me and I would have had it within the hour. Dope, speed, ecstasy – any 'party drug' is completely acceptable on that circuit. But heroin, or crack for that matter, is the last great taboo as far as drugs are concerned. It doesn't matter how rock and roll you are, you just don't ask for it. And you especially don't ask for it when you are a 31-year-old mother of three.

By now I was getting extremely desperate. I went back into the dressing-room and sat on a chair, wondering what to do next. I needed something to keep me going, to stop me from withdrawing. I had three tabs of ecstasy on me, which I had planned to take with Danny at the party following the gig. I took the pills from my bag and laid them on the dressing-table. Maybe these would make me feel better. Maybe, with any luck, the ecstasy would be laced with a little smack.

I took a glass from the table and started to crush the pills up, then chopped them into a fine powder with my credit card. As a seasoned drug-taker, I knew that taken this way the drug would enter my system more quickly, giving me a greater and more intense rush than if I swallowed them.

'What the hell are you doing?' asked Zoë.

'Sorting myself out, of course!' was my reply.

'Do you really think you should be taking ecstasy? You've already taken smack. You're going to really mess yourself up.'

I ignored her, rolled up a banknote and leant over the three white lines of ecstasy I had neatly drawn on the dressing-table.

It was a huge mistake. As I snorted the first line of ecstasy my nose began to burn, by the second the sensation was even more extreme, as if I had inhaled a thousand shards of broken glass. I should have blown my nose and washed the poison from my nostrils, but instead I inhaled deeply . . . As I did so, and the drug took hold of me, I was gripped by a spasm of pain so intense that I thought my brain was about to explode. Holding my head in my hands, I fell to the floor. I had never felt pain like it, and I really believed that I was about to die. I started to scream. Zoë was standing over me and panicking. 'Help! Someone help us! We need a doctor, we need a fucking ambulance! We need help, now!' And with that I blacked out.

I don't recall much after that. I remember somehow getting back to the hotel in a car. I remember, as I slipped in and out of consciousness, watching the lights of Paris flash before me as the car sped through the city. I remember lying on the bathroom floor of my hotel room, a doctor coming, and hearing a muffled conversation from the bedroom. I remember Zoë stroking my head, trying to tell me that I was going to be OK. And I remember being given an injection, and after that – nothing.

What actually happened, I learnt later, was that help did come. When the promoter – the same one I had asked to get heroin for me just half an hour before – heard Zoë's screams, he ran straight to the dressing-room and, taking one look at me, wanted to call for an ambulance. Apparently, when I came round momentarily, I refused. It wasn't that bad, I kept telling them. I'd be fine once I was back at the hotel and in bed. Calls were made, and a doctor, one known for his discretion in such matters, was contacted. He told them to get me back to the hotel, where he would meet us. A private car was ordered, and Zoë took me back. She got me into the room and tried to get me to lie on the bed, but I wanted to be in the bathroom because I was starting to feel sick. I was too weak to stand or even sit on the loo, which is how I came to be curled up on the cold tiles of the bathroom floor. The doctor came within an hour, although it seemed like an eternity to Zoë, and having found out what I had taken, gave me an injection – to this day I don't know what it was. They then put me to bed, and within fifteen minutes I was asleep.

All this time Danny had been unaware of what had happened. When I blacked out he was already on stage, and it was decided that it was best not to tell him until after the concert. It was an important gig for the band. There were a lot of press there, including a reporter from the *NME*, who had come all the way from London to see the band. No one really knew how ill I was at that stage anyway. Zoë and the promoter played it down, telling anyone who asked that I had left the concert because I had overdone it. When Danny came off stage and was told the news he rushed back to the hotel.

When I woke at around seven in the morning, Danny was sitting at the end of the bed. He had been there all night. He didn't want to sleep in case something happened to me. He was scared that I might have a fit or, worse still, that I might stop breathing. He looked shattered.

'Where am I?' I asked groggily. My head was still hurting, my vision was blurred, my mouth was dry and I had no recollection of what had happened to me.

'It's OK, you're here with me in Paris. You're OK now.' He reached over and took my hand.

'I thought I was dead.'

'You were very lucky, you could have died.'

13

'But I'm OK . . . I'm OK . . .'

'Yes, you are, you are OK, but you were lucky, you were very lucky. I could have lost you, you know.'

I had been lucky, very lucky, and Danny, more than anyone, was aware of that. As he sat there at the end of my bed through the night, waiting for me to come round, the enormity of what had happened hit him extremely hard. So, we took drugs – most people we knew took drugs, it was part of our world. And there had been times when we had both overdone it and had paid the consequences the following day. But nothing like this had ever happened before, nothing quite so extreme.

'I think really we have to knock this on the head,' he said to me.

'Knock what on the head?'

'This . . . the drugs . . . the heroin. It's got to stop. *You've* got to stop this now. Enough is enough. We've got a young family, three kids, a baby – we just can't carry on like this. Look what you are doing to yourself.'

'I don't know what you're talking about. I haven't got a problem, you know I haven't. I only do it occasionally. And it was the ecstasy that made me ill, not the heroin. I was silly, it was a silly mistake, I shouldn't have mixed the E with the smack. It was stupid. If I hadn't done that I would have been fine.'

'You're not fine. Look at you. You could have died. This has got to stop. Your habit has to stop here, it's got really bad. You know it has and you know what I am saying.' Still holding on to his hand, I turned my head away from him. I couldn't face looking him in the eye.

Now here I am on the train home, feeling terrible in every way. Thanks to me everyone's weekend has been ruined – Zoë's birthday, Danny's big night, our time together – and now we are coming home a day early, our trip cut short. I want to go home, but if I am honest I just can't face it. I can't face the children, I can't face my mother, but I have to.

We arrive home at Stratford Villas, and they are all there waiting for me – my mother, Daisy, Alfie and little Frankie asleep in the nanny's arms. 'Pearl, you look awful,' my mother tells me. 'Didn't you have a good time? I thought you were supposed to be having a rest.'

It's early evening now. My mother has left, the children are all in bed, and that's where I should be too, as Danny keeps telling me – in bed, resting. But I don't want to go to sleep and I don't want to rest. I know what I want and so I pick up the phone. The dealer is round within the hour, just as he said he would be, just as he always is.

Two months later I am in rehab.

2

See Her Riding In

To an outsider, looking in, it must have seemed as though I had it all back then. I had fulfilled my lifelong ambition of making it in the music industry and had gained relative success and recognition within that world as the lead singer of the Britpop indie band Powder. I had the rock star boyfriend, who was riding high with his own band Supergrass at the time, and I had three beautiful and healthy children: Frankie, my newborn son, Alfie, who was two, and ten-year-old Daisy, my daughter from a previous relationship.

We lived in a large stucco house in north London, which we had bought two years earlier. Set in one of Camden's more affluent streets, it was the kind of property that wouldn't have looked out of place in the pages of an interior design magazine. We drove nice cars, took exotic holidays, ate in expensive restaurants and shopped for clothes in designer stores. Though we were by no means multimillionaires, we were rich enough not to have to worry about money, and so never thought twice about spending it.

When we weren't at home with the children, Danny and I liked to socialise, and we had a wide circle of friends, some of whom just happened to be famous. We mixed with other musicians from the Britpop scene, were friends with actors, models and others from the worlds of fashion and film. We went to glamorous parties, both here and abroad, we attended awards ceremonies and industry events and found ourselves invited to premieres and openings. We liked going to gigs and concerts and in the summer months would spend our weekends at music festivals. It was, for the most part, just one, long, never-ending party.

I was living the kind of life that most people can only dream of and with so much going my way, personally, professionally, financially and socially, I suppose I should have been happy. In fact, I was anything but. I was utterly miserable, on the very brink of an emotional breakdown. On the outside I may have been smiling, I may have looked as though I was having the time of my life, but inside I was in a state of turmoil, struggling to come to terms with the demons that haunted my every waking hour. There wasn't a night that I didn't go to bed in tears during this period, not a morning when I didn't wake up consumed by feelings of despair, fear, guilt and self-loathing.

Looking back now, I can see that I had a gilded existence, but that's all it was, for if you scratched the surface enough, peeled away the gilt and the gloss, all was not what it seemed. Beneath the bright, shiny veneer my life was extremely dark, the reason being that I was hopelessly and perilously addicted to drugs. Of course, I didn't see that at the time. I couldn't see that my addiction was casting a long shadow over the rest of my life. Like the fool I was, I believed that drugs were the answer to my pain, not the cause of it, and as things got progressively worse for me I would rely on them more and more. I turned to drugs – my powders, be they brown or white – when what I should have done then was turn to someone and ask for the help I so desperately needed.

In the worlds that Danny and I moved in, recreational drug use was commonplace. A lot of the people we mixed with, either socially or professionally, took drugs, that's just how it was then. You'd share a joint with a friend at the end of the day to help you unwind. You'd pop a tab of ecstasy at a club or a gig with your mates to get you into the spirit of the night. You would go to a dinner party and be offered a line of cocaine before you had even started on the main course. Taking drugs was as sociably acceptable within our circle as opening a bottle of wine, or smoking a cigarette. With the exception of, perhaps, my parents, most people we were close to during that time knew that Danny and I liked our drugs. We made no secret of it. Amongst our clique we felt comfortable using. We would openly smoke cannabis in public, use coke and speed in front of our friends, take ecstasy if we were in the mood. I would happily follow a virtual stranger into a loo in order to take a line of cocaine at a party if it was offered to me. Indeed, such was my appetite for drugs, and especially cocaine, that I earned myself the rather unflattering nickname of Dyson, after the all-powerful vacuum cleaner. But whilst I may have had a reputation that preceded me when it came to 'partying', as we called it then, even our friends didn't know at the time the full extent of my drug addiction.

They didn't know that I bought and used heroin. Or that I frequently smoked it at home on my own. They weren't aware that I did this most days of the week, just to get through the day. As far as they were concerned I didn't have a 'problem',

I just used drugs the way we all did, 'recreationally' – at night, on a special occasion, maybe over a weekend, when we went to a party. By this stage, however, my drug use was far from being recreational. I was dependent on drugs to such an extent that if I didn't take them I became physically ill.

There were only two people in my life then who were aware of my addiction to heroin – Zoë and, of course, Danny. They knew I took the drug and was fast becoming hooked on it. Zoë knew because she was my best friend and I had confided in her. Danny knew because I lived with him and I had used with him. But even they were not aware of just how increasingly dependent I was on it by this stage. Like the true addict I was, I managed, for a time, to conceal my habit, even from those who were closest to me. With Zoë it was straightforward. When I was on one of my binges I just wouldn't call or see her. I would excuse these absences by pretending that I had been too busy with the children, with work commitments, or with Danny, to contact her. It was easy with Danny too. During the late 1990s his career had really taken off, unlike mine. We were in the midst of the heady days of Cool Britannia, when people couldn't get enough of the new British sound, and although Supergrass were not exactly in the same league as bands such as Oasis or Blur, they had, nevertheless, produced a couple of award-winning albums and were big on the scene at the time. When they weren't holed up in the studio in London, they were constantly on the road, performing at gigs all over the world. So although we were close and committed, for the best part of a year we lived quite separate lives, spending weeks at a time away from each other. I was in London with the children, keeping up the home front, whilst he toured the world, performing. As painful and difficult as these times apart were, I couldn't complain. It was thanks to Danny and the success of his band that we were able to afford the life we had.

But it was during these separations that I really fell victim to drugs. Maybe I was trying to fill the void, over-indulging to ease the pain of our separations. Maybe I was just using these times apart as an opportunity to take as much heroin as I could without constraint. To this day I can't really say what the reason was. All I do know is that my addiction to heroin had overtaken my life.

I didn't use every day of the week – I could go for months without it when I wanted to – but when I was using I didn't know where to draw the line. I would take the drug for days on end, and during this time I wouldn't sleep and I wouldn't eat – I couldn't, for as anyone who has ever taken the drug knows, it is impossible to do either when you are on smack.

I kept my heroin use away from my friends because I knew they would disapprove. Whilst the majority of them were pretty open-minded and many were not adverse to drug-taking themselves, no one took heroin. You just didn't go there. Heroin retained its stigma as being one of the most dangerous substances known to man. Everyone knew the risks involved with taking it; everyone knew how highly and physically addictive it was; everyone knew that it wasn't something you could toy with, a drug that you could just take or leave. Everyone seemed to know this, apart from me. Because I didn't use every day, because I could go without the drug for months at a time, I really believed that I had my use under control. I wasn't an addict, I couldn't be, because I could stop and start again when

I wanted. I didn't look or act like an addict either. I wasn't so desperate for the drug that I stole from my friends and family, I wasn't jacking up in some council flat on an estate, or visiting some skanky crack house late at night. I just took the drug when I wanted to, when I felt like it, when I wanted that little high. I was in control. I was on top of it. That's what I told myself over and over again, convincing myself that I was fine, and to a certain extent I was.

Despite my predilection for the drug I managed to live a normal life. I took care of the children and spent time with them. I looked after my new baby, played with my two-year-old son, and helped Daisy with her homework. I made their breakfast, often did the school run, made their tea and supper. I ran the house, keeping it tidy, and made improvements to it. On top of this I still managed to work. I was writing new material, coming up with ideas for the band, always thinking about music. There were meetings to go to and telephone calls that had to be made. I maintained a social life and went out at night with my friends. I visited my parents, went shopping, out to lunch. I took pride in my appearance, always making an effort with my clothes and make-up. When Danny was home I would entertain, cooking large lunches for our family and friends.

Because I was able to maintain this routine and to function normally, people had no idea what was going on behind the scenes. They didn't know that once the older children were off at school and at nursery, and Frankie had gone off with the nanny, I was reaching for the telephone in order to call my dealer. They weren't aware that I spent days on end smoking heroin alone in my bedroom and that I would do this for four or five days on end. They would have been shocked to find out that I smoked heroin in the house when the children were there and was often high when they were in my care. They didn't know, because I didn't want them to. I went to great lengths to hide my habit from everyone around me.

If I smoked during the day in the house, I would open all the windows and light scented candles to disguise the smell. If I had been up all night getting high, I always made sure that I was there to make the children's breakfast in the morning, no matter how ill I felt. If someone called me for a chat and I was using, I still managed to sound lucid and together.

But it was all a charade really. I may have functioned normally, but that's all I was doing – just functioning, not living. I may have been there with the children, physically there, but I wasn't there in spirit. As they sat and played or chatted away to me, I would listen half-heartedly. It wasn't that I didn't want to be involved with them, I just found it a strain. I had no energy, no enthusiasm for anything. The countless projects I worked on never came to anything. I would talk up an idea for days when I was high, but that's all it ever amounted to – just talk. When I was on drugs, I wasn't in a state to put any of these great ideas of mine into fruition. When I was off them, I didn't have the drive to follow anything through. I would miss meetings and appointments because I had either forgotten to go to them or I just couldn't face people. I'd cancel studio sessions and interviews, and was forever letting people down. I kept in contact with my friends, but I was never really there for any of them. I let Zoë down on so many occasions that it got to the point where she gave up relying on me for anything. Although I made an effort with my appearance, there was no escaping the fact that I was losing my looks. I had dropped so much weight that when I undressed my naked body repelled me. I was nothing more than a skeleton. Dark circles had formed under my eyes, and my skin, which had always been clear during my teens, was now covered in spots.

By the middle of 1999, after three years of using heroin off and on, I finally started to see that I had a problem. Although I was loath to admit that it had anything to do with my drug use, I knew that something was wrong. I was so profoundly unhappy, I found no joy in my life whatsoever. Not even Danny or the children, all of whom I loved to bits, could make me feel any better. I had lost my zest for life and couldn't see how I was ever going to get it back. I would lie on my bed for hours on end, staring listlessly at the ceiling. I would burst into tears for no reason, and sit there sobbing through the day and night. I found it hard to get up in the morning and was unable to sleep unless I had taken a heavy cocktail of sleeping pills and tranquilisers. Despite everything I had, I hated my life and I hated myself.

I couldn't understand why I felt like this, I didn't know what was causing this pain. All I knew was that I wanted to rid myself of it, and the only thing that seemed to make me feel any better was heroin. The cause of my agony was also its only cure.

3

Deep-fried

They say that everyone has their drug of choice, and mine was always heroin. Although I have experimented with most mind-altering substances over the years – legal and otherwise – nothing ever came close to how I felt when I was on that drug: the sheer intensity of the high it gave me, the sudden surge of warmth and happiness that enveloped my body once I had taken it, the sense of pleasure it produced as it coursed through my system. Within minutes of that first hit I was transported to another world, lifted to a higher, more spiritual plane. I felt free, released from the drudgery of my daily existence. I felt weightless, up there with the angels, floating on my own little opiate cloud. I was enlightened. I was euphoric.

But the thing I liked about heroin most of all was the fact that on it I felt no pain, either physical or emotional. It was my own private, beautiful anaesthetic that could be administered at my whim throughout the day. One puff was all it took to make the world a better place. Any pain I had, any anxiety I felt, any issues I faced would all disappear once I started using. On it I didn't have a single care in the world, and I liked it that way. It made life bearable, and if you took enough if it, for a while it even made life beautiful. I felt protected, safe in my lovely little bubble. That's why I took it.

Some people like the odd glass of wine to get them through the day. Others find solace in a bottle of spirits. Some people like smoking dope, because it makes them laugh and feel happy. Others prefer the 'rush' they get from drugs such as cocaine or speed. For a great proportion of the population a cigarette is enough to get them going. But for me it was always smack. I didn't need a drug to give me energy, I already had far too much of that as it was. I had never been one for alcohol: I just didn't, and still don't, like the taste, and I certainly didn't like the way it made me feel. What I wanted was a drug that desensitised me from the world, without taking me away from it. That's what I thought heroin did for me. How mistaken I was.

Although I didn't become addicted to drugs until my mid-twenties, since my early teens they had always been in my life. At the age of thirteen I smoked my first joint, at fifteen I took my first line of cocaine, and by the time I was eighteen, and hit the London club scene, I had began to dabble with ecstasy. This might sound alarming to some, but for my generation, where I came from, experimenting with drugs was just part of our rite of passage. Taking a drug for the first time was no different from having your first kiss, your first drink, your first sexual encounter, your first heartbreak. It was all part and parcel of growing up. And, in any case, when I first started experimenting with drugs I wasn't that into them. I didn't do drugs to get stoned, or high, or out of it. For me it was all about doing something illicit and naughty, something my parents would have disapproved of. That's what gave me my kick, my thrill. When I reached my late teens my approach to drug-taking changed and I started to like the way they made me feel. Looking back now, I think that one of the main reasons for this was that I didn't drink, so I started substituting drugs for alcohol.

Whilst my friends would sit around drinking and getting merry, I would smoke copious amounts of dope so as to be on a level with them. If we were out clubbing or partying I would rely on ecstasy to give me the lift that I needed. By this point in my life I had developed quite an appetite for drugs, particularly cannabis and E, and yet even though I used quite regularly, and would often buy my own supplies, I was by no means addicted. I could take them or leave them quite easily. It wasn't until I discovered heroin that I developed a problem. From that very first hit, as the fumes took hold of my body and soul, I knew that I wanted to take this drug more and more, and I realised that I could easily become addicted to it. Nothing I had ever tried before had made me feel so beautiful and happy, so carefree. I had, at last, found my drug.

Throughout the years that I have been clean from drugs, the many counselling and therapy sessions I have sat through, the group meetings I have attended, I have tried to understand why I became an addict. I have undergone intensive therapy sessions, consulted psychiatrists, psychics and healers even, and asked myself this question over and over again. I have looked back into my past and tried to discover who or what led me down this path of self-destruction. It would be so much easier to lay the blame at someone else's door, to find some trauma or event in my past that resulted in my ultimate downfall, but the fact is that it was all down to me. I was the one who chose to be this way.

I may not have become addicted to drugs until my twenties, until I started using heroin, but I can see now that I started to veer off my path in my early teens. I was rebellious by nature and despised the idea of having to conform or toe the line. The very idea of playing by the rules filled me with a sense of abject horror. I didn't like being told what to do, or how to behave. I didn't appreciate it when people told me what was good for me and what wasn't. I was determined to discover these things for myself, to learn my own lessons in life.

I had a very conventional, middle-class upbringing. My parents, who are still married, worked in the rag trade, and by most people's standards we were comfortably off. We lived in nice houses in and around London, took family holidays, and my two older brothers and I were sent to good schools. Although both my parents worked, they were always there for us and tried to ensure that we had a happy and stable childhood. They weren't disciplinarians but they set ground rules and taught us the importance of right and wrong. When I was a small child I listened to my parents and did what I was told, but as I grew up, and developed a mind of my own, I was determined to do things my way. As the youngest child and the only girl in the family I enjoyed a lot more freedom than my brothers did and I took full advantage of this. I was wild and I was wilful. If my parents or my teachers would tell me to do one thing I would do the exact opposite. I was forever up to mischief, climbing out of my bedroom window when I should have been doing my homework, playing truant from school, answering back when I should have kept quiet. I seemed to spend a lot of those years hanging out in parks and at people's houses when their parents were out. We'd watch movies, smoke the odd cigarette or joint, hang out with boys and hold parties.

In my early teens I had a lot of friends and liked to socialise, but I never belonged to a gang as such. The fact that I had two older brothers gave me a degree of confidence that a lot of girls my age didn't share. I looked up to my brothers, learnt from them and quite early on realised that I didn't have to follow the herd. My taste in music, literature and films was always quite alternative, and I abhorred the very idea of 'fashion'. I remember going to a birthday party one night, when I can't have been more than twelve, and seeing a girl there wearing an identical dress to mine. I was appalled, and when I got home that night I told my mother that I would never wear the dress again. From that moment onwards I set about customising my clothes. I would sit in my room at weekends cutting sleeves off shirts and dresses, sewing on buttons and beads as I listened to music. I didn't want to look like everyone else, I wanted to be my own person. I didn't see the point in following trends just for the sake of it.

My behaviour during my teenage years exasperated both my parents, and on one occasion my recklessness resulted in my mother having to be hospitalised. We were having an argument one afternoon because I had just declared to her that I wanted to go off 'travelling' to get out of her hair. She tried to reason with me, but I was having none of it.

'If that's what you want to do then, just go,' she said, at the end of her tether. 'But you will need a suitcase if you are going anywhere.'

I knew that she was trying to call my bluff and was annoyed. 'Yes, I will!' I said defiantly. 'Can I borrow one?'

My mother decided to play me at my own game and climbed on to a step-ladder to fetch me a case from a shelf at the top of a cupboard, but lost her footing and fell. She fractured a rib, punctured a lung and was bedridden for over a week. Even though I knew I was responsible for her accident, I refused to apologise.

My parents tried to be patient with me and get to the root of my teenage rebellion, but they were on a losing wicket. If they tried to give me one of their talks, I just didn't want to know. I would go off and do something to annoy them on purpose, such as cut off all my hair, get a tattoo or walk out of school at the age of sixteen, declaring that I'd had enough of it.

Unlike my brothers, who were both academic and hard-working, I had never enjoyed school. Although I was bright, I found it tedious. I didn't concentrate in lessons and was always far more interested in what was going on outside the classroom window than what was going on inside. There was a world out there I was desperate to explore. I didn't need to be told about it by my teachers, I wanted to discover it for myself. My parents weren't surprised by my decision to leave school, but they were disappointed, especially since I didn't have a single qualification to my name. Realising that there was nothing they could do to change my mind, they gave in, but I was told, in no uncertain terms, that if that was my decision then I would have to get a job and support myself if I wanted to stay under their roof. I didn't mind. Even though I hated school I wasn't work-shy. This was one attribute I had inherited from my parents. I liked the idea of having a job and earning my own money. I just no longer wanted to sit in a classroom learning about life: I wanted to live it.

Leaving school without having passed any exams didn't exactly enhance my career prospects, and so I embarked on a series of the most mundane jobs in the history of employment, from working in a shoe shop to answering the telephone at a local beauty salon, but I wasn't that bothered. I was enjoying life and lived it to the full. I revelled in my newfound independence. I liked the fact that I could do what I wanted, when I wanted; that I no longer had to answer to anyone. By day, at work, I may have been bored, but at night I made sure that I always had a good time. I had a new circle of friends and we would spend our evenings together, either getting stoned at home or going out clubbing till the early hours of the morning. I quickly immersed myself in this group, forming close friendships within it, and it was on this scene that I met two of my greatest friends in life – Zoë Grace and a young musician called Gavin Rossdale.

I first met Zoë, who was an aspiring artist, when I was seventeen and out clubbing one night at the Limelight, a nightclub in north London. To be honest I wasn't sure I liked her very much at the beginning. She was four years older than I was, and I remember her being very standoffish to me that night. But as I began to see more of her on my social circuit we warmed to each other, and once we discovered that we shared a mutual fascination with the spiritual world we became the closest of friends and would spend hours together discussing psychic phenomena and giving each other Tarot readings.

Gavin and I met at the WAG club later that year. With his

long curly hair, the crucifix round his neck and his leather trousers he resembled a young Jim Morrison and I was instantly drawn to him. We hit it off straight away. He told me he was in a band and introduced me to his friends that night. After that we became inseparable. Although he had a girlfriend at the time, and I was seeing one of his friends, we were extremely close. We would meet for coffee most mornings and spend our weekends out clubbing or going to gigs. He was the first man I had formed a significant friendship with, and I loved the fact that he was part of my life.

By the age of nineteen, after three years of working life, I decided that I had grown weary of London and wanted to travel. I booked a trip to Israel and Egypt, on the advice of a friend who had just returned from there. When I told my parents about my plans they weren't particularly enthusiastic. They were pleased I was going away but were concerned by my decision to travel on my own. However, there was nothing they could do to dissuade me. I was making my own way in the world now and had decided that it was time I saw a little of it. Unlike my parents, I wasn't concerned at the prospect of travelling on my own: for me it just added to the adventure. I had never had a problem meeting people and just days after arriving in Israel I found myself a band of travelling companions. Together we headed to the Sinai desert, and it was here that I met a young man who was about to have a profound effect on the rest of my life.

His name was Bronner and he was from New York. When we met he was hanging out with a gang of your archetypal travellers with their long hair and deep tans and their hippy clothes and jewellery. They had been travelling round the world for a couple of months and were full of stories about their adventures. Bronner wasn't the best looking of the group, but he was easily the most attractive to me. I thought he was cute with his long, sandy-coloured hair and his hazel eyes, but the thing I liked about him most was that he appeared to be so worldly. He was only 23, but to me, coming from my middle-class London background, he seemed to have done so much with his life already. He would dazzle me with stories of his trip and his life back in New York City. He seemed so cool and so laid back – a free and kindred spirit – and it wasn't long before we embarked on a love affair.

However much I was into Bronner during those few months together, in the back of my mind I always considered our relationship to be nothing more than a holiday fling. Even though we had pledged our love to one another, and I was happy when we were together, I knew he wasn't 'the one' and that our affair would end when I returned to England that winter. We lived on different sides of the world, after all, had little in common other than our shared experiences travelling together, and at nineteen I certainly had no intention of settling down just yet. So when he suggested towards the end of the trip that he should return with me to London when my holiday came to an end, I admit that I was rather taken aback.

'Come on, Pearl, it will be fun,' he said to me. 'You know I love you and want to be with you. Why should we stop now? Why should it end here?'

Of course, there were plenty of reasons why it should have ended there and then, but I was just too young and naïve to see them at that moment in time, too foolish to leave things as and where they were, and so in November we flew back to England together. When I told my parents that I was moving out of home and in with this virtual stranger, they were against the idea, but once again they couldn't do anything about it. When they tried to talk me round and get me to see sense, I refused to listen to them. Despite my initial reluctance to have anything more to do with Bronner once the holiday came to an end, I was flattered that he wanted to be with me and determined that we would be together and that it would all work out. But within just a matter of weeks of getting back to London I knew that I had made a huge mistake.

Back at home, away from the sun, the beach and the gloss of a holiday, I began to see Bronner in a whole new light. We had moved into a tiny flat in St John's Wood that was owned by a family friend. Thanks to my father, Bronner found himself a job, and I had started to get some modelling work, having signed up with an agency, but as we slipped into our domestic life together it soon became apparent that we weren't compatible.

Bronner wasn't the man I thought he was. Far from being the happy-go-lucky free spirit I had met travelling, I soon discovered that there was another side to him. I felt that he was extremely possessive of me, to the point where it was suffocating rather than flattering. He was also controlling and prone to mood swings. It didn't help that I had my own life in London and I got the impression that he was suspicious of my friendships – especially those with Gavin and Zoë. There would be times when if I was going out to meet up with them he would make his displeasure all too evident, to the extent that I felt under pressure to cancel.

I was beginning to find our relationship unbearably stifling.

After so many years of fighting for my independence, suddenly it was completely stripped away from me. He didn't want me to go out without him, he didn't like me seeing other people, he didn't approve of me spending the night out dancing with my friends. After a while I felt I couldn't do anything without Bronner's permission, and as I began to realise the terrible mistake I had made and it dawned on me that I wasn't in love with him, things between us got progressively worse.

My family and friends were horrified by the effect it was having on me but didn't know what to do. They tried to persuade me to leave him, but I couldn't. Bronner's behaviour had worn me down and I had no strength, no energy to fight back. Whenever I told him I wanted to end the relationship he would either talk me round or else threaten me with the consequences of leaving.

'You have to get rid of him, Pearl!' Zoë said to me. 'Look at you, you are a mess, he's destroying your life.'

Gavin, who made no bones about his feelings for Bronner, agreed and during those months became my shoulder to cry on. Desperate to escape Bronner, I would spend hours with Gavin at his flat. Once my tears were dry, to ease my nerves and my pain, I would sit there on his sofa smoking a spliff, trying to make myself feel better. In getting stoned I could shut out the reality of my situation for a couple of hours at least.

It wasn't until June 1988 that my relationship with Bronner finally came to an end. By a stroke of luck his visa had run out, so he had no choice other than to pack his bags and return to the States, at least for a couple of months. In fact we had both come to the conclusion by that stage that it was better that he didn't return. Neither of us could cope with the constant bickering and fights, and this seemed the right time to make the break. The day he left I was so relieved; I felt I had reclaimed my life again. I could do what I wanted to do, see who I wanted to see and be who I wanted to be. I felt as if I had been reborn. It was a fresh start and a new beginning, and I truly believed that I would never see him again. But just three weeks later something happened that put paid to that. I discovered that I was two months pregnant.

From the moment I saw the pregnancy test I knew that I was going to keep the baby. It never occurred to me not to. I knew quite a few girls of my age who had had terminations, but I didn't want to go down that route. I was pregnant and I was going to have my baby. Yes, I was young, and I didn't have a job, or a man in my life, but we would survive, somehow. There were plenty of other young girls out there, far less fortunate than me, who coped. I was nervous telling my parents, imagining that they would try to talk me round and get me to change my mind, but they didn't. They supported my decision and promised that they would do everything they could to help. In retrospect I think they had concluded that having a child of my own, someone to look after, might stabilise me, give me the grounding and sense of responsibility I had always lacked. And they were right. As soon as I discovered I was having a baby I hung up my dancing shoes, stopped going out at night and gave up taking drugs. My attitude towards my life took a dramatic turn for the better.

I certainly didn't want Bronner back in my life just because I was pregnant, and I had already come to the decision to raise the baby on my own. All the same I was conscious that I should do the right thing by him and let him know he was going to be a father, so I called him in America a week later. I had always assumed that when I told him he would either insist that I had a termination, or tell me that he didn't want anything to do with the child. But that wasn't the reaction I got.

'That's amazing!' he trilled. 'We're going to have a baby!'

'You're not angry?'

'No! Why would I be? Look, whatever happens between you and me, I will support you and the child, no matter what. So we need to talk this through, but face to face, not on the phone.'

Because Bronner's UK visa had expired he couldn't come back to England, so it was arranged that I would meet him in Miami, where he was staying with his family, the following week. I hadn't planned to go for long, a couple of days at the most. After we had talked it all through and made arrangements for our baby's future and maintenance, I would return to England alone. But a fortnight later I was still there. Bronner and his mother, a kind but formidable character, started to talk me round.

'Look, Pearl, let's try again,' he said. 'We have to stop thinking about ourselves and think about our child and its future. It's better that it has two parents, you know it is.'

'He's right, Pearl,' his mother said. 'It isn't easy raising a child as it is, it's even harder when there is just one of you. You've got to think about the baby now and put your child first.' And so I did.

We were married a month later by a lake in Miami. I was by then three months pregnant and was dressed in a hideous blue and white polka-dot dress. My parents flew out for the ceremony. They didn't like Bronner and weren't convinced that I was making the right decision, but I had made up my mind. The baby comes first, I kept telling them. If Bronner and I were going to raise the child together in England I was going to have to marry him, otherwise he couldn't stay in the country. I certainly had no intention of moving to the States. If I was going to be with him and do this, then I wanted my friends and family around me to support me. Marrying Bronner was the last thing that I wanted to do, but I felt I didn't really have any option, and so with a faint heart I made my vows to him standing by that lake and we were pronounced man and wife. On our return to London my parents threw a large party for us on the River Thames. All my family and friends were invited and were kind enough to attend. I was by now five months pregnant and wore a lace dress and an incredibly brave face.

4

Daisy

Most of my friends were surprised by my decision to keep the baby. I had gained quite a reputation for my wild behaviour, and few could see me settling down. Before I had got together with Bronner there was nothing I liked more in life than going out and partying. I was always the first to arrive, always the last to leave and always 'up for it', and although I didn't drink I did like my drugs. If I wasn't sitting around my flat getting stoned, then I'd be out dancing till dawn having taken ecstasy. I was your ultimate party girl, and few could see me slipping into the role of a doting mother – but I could and I did, and from the moment my daughter came into my life I was completely devoted to her.

Daisy Lowe was born at the Portland Hospital, in London, on 27 January 1989. I hadn't intended to have her privately – on our meagre incomes Bronner and I certainly couldn't have afforded that luxury, and I wasn't prepared to ask my parents to help out. But towards the end of my pregnancy I became extremely ill with toxaemia, and for a while it was touch and go. Fortunately, at the insistence of my father, I had taken out a health insurance policy and had always kept up with my payments no matter how broke I was, so when it became clear just how severe the condition was, my doctor admitted me to the private clinic just before her birth.

I fell in love with Daisy the moment the midwife put her in my arms for the first time. She weighed six pounds twelve ounces and was simply the most beautiful little thing I had seen in my entire life. To me she was perfect in every way, with her tiny fingers and toes. She had the most exquisite heart-shaped face, and eyes the size of saucers. I couldn't believe that anything this beautiful could really belong to me. The love I immediately felt for her during those first few moments together overwhelmed me. I had never loved anyone or anything as much in my entire life. I felt as if I had been given the best present imaginable, and I couldn't take my eyes off her.

It would be fair to say that most people who knew me just assumed that I would get bored with Daisy once the novelty of having a child had worn off and the daily routine and sleepless nights had kicked in, but in fact I took to motherhood quite easily. I even surprised myself. Before I had Daisy I knew very little about children, let alone babies. I didn't know how to change a nappy, I'd never held or bathed a tiny baby, and it certainly never occurred to me that they didn't sleep through the night! I was a quick learner, though, and by the time we brought Daisy home to a flat we had rented on the Shirland Road, in west London, I had taken to my new role with gusto.

Overnight I transformed myself from the tearaway teenager I had once been into a domestic goddess. Whereas in the past I never got up until three in the afternoon if I could possibly help it, I now found myself hovering over my daughter's cot at three in the morning with her bottle in hand in case she woke for a feed. My flat, once a pit of dirty dishes and party debris, now gleamed. My bedroom floor was no longer littered with clothes; instead everything was washed, ironed and either folded or hung. When Daisy moved on to solid foods I learnt to cook and took pride in preparing all her meals. I even took to dusting and hoovering, and I loved every moment of it.

Bronner and I were by no means on the breadline, but financially things were a struggle for us at first. I don't think I had any conception before I had Daisy of just how much babies cost. Fortunately, Bronner had managed to find a job, and with the little money I got from the state we managed to get by. We were also lucky in that I had the love and support of my parents. They helped out as much as they could, paying for some nursery furniture for Daisy and giving us money to buy clothes for her. Though they were keen for me to stand on my own two feet and take responsibility for Daisy, they were also determined that their first grandchild was going to have a lovely life no matter what our circumstances. To be honest, they both fell hopelessly in love with their grand-daughter, and as she grew up and turned into a bright and enchanting child, I think they felt that in Daisy they had, at last, got the little girl they had always longed for. She was everything I wasn't. My older brothers too would use any excuse to come over to play with Daisy, lavishing love and attention on her.

From the outset Zoë and Gavin were extremely supportive as well. Unlike other friends who, when I discovered I was pregnant, tried to talk me out of having Daisy, they had backed my decision to keep her. They had rallied round me during my pregnancy, and so within days of her birth I made them both her godparents. Zoë was a natural choice as a godmother. Not only was she my best friend and adored children, but with her spiritual beliefs and outlook on life I knew that she would always look out for Daisy's moral welfare, which was important to me.

Gavin's involvement with Daisy, I have to admit, took me by surprise. He was very busy with his music career at that stage and he looked and acted every inch the rock star, so while I knew that he would always be there for us, I never expected him to be quite so hands-on. But Gavin took his duties as godfather extremely seriously. He came to the hospital to see Daisy the day she was born. He would pop by the flat as often as he could to see her and was constantly ringing to see how she was. Later, when she was at school, he would accompany me to parents' evenings and always came to her school plays if he was around. He would take her off for walks to Primrose Hill and Camden Market, where he would buy her little presents. He was always offering to baby-sit for me during the day, and when he did I would return home to find the flat turned upside down by their high jinks.

For the first year of Daisy's life I had no social life to speak of. I saw friends during the day, but I didn't have a night-life – not that I cared. I had been doing that scene for so long by that stage that I felt I'd had my fill of it. All I wanted was to be at home with my baby. I didn't want to go to nightclubs, I was far happier taking my daughter to baby groups or for walks in the park in her pram. My mother frequently offered to baby-sit for me, so I could have a night off, but I rarely took her up on her offer. I didn't want to go out, that world was over for me now. I had been introduced to a new one that I found far more rewarding. And so for a time my life was pretty perfect, and I think I can truthfully say that it was one of the happiest periods of my life. There was just one blot on the horizon, and that was Bronner.

Marriage hadn't made our relationship any easier; if anything it became more strained than ever. Eventually it reached such a low point that at times I found it uncomfortable even being in the same room as him. The relief I felt each morning when he left for work was palpable, as was the feeling of dread that hit me every time I heard his key turn in the lock when he returned home at night. Having Daisy around hadn't smoothed out our differences, it just accentuated them. I had always hoped that her presence in our lives might soften him, but sadly it didn't. He appeared unsettled by the time and attention I gave to Daisy and although I knew that he loved her, the pressure of caring for a young baby made him more stressed and irritable with both of us.

He may have thought when we married that a baby would bring us closer together, but it can, in fact, do the exact opposite. We had nothing in common other than our child, and we both knew that. We had nothing else to talk about when we were alone together, nothing to share other than frosty silences or angry words. We were two people leading separate lives under the same very tiny roof, and it wasn't comfortable for either of us.

For a time I tried to put a brave face on things, assuring friends and family that everything was fine between us. They weren't fooled – the only one I was kidding was myself. Even though I knew that I wasn't happy, I didn't want the relationship to end. For Daisy's sake I tried to make a go of it, tried to make it work, but it was no use. As the months went on,

Bronner became increasingly hostile and antagonistic towards me. If he wasn't shouting and screaming at me, then he would ignore me for days at a time. Zoë and Gavin repeatedly urged me to leave him, but I couldn't see a way out. I had neither the energy or the strength to stand up to him. If I said I was leaving he would beg and plead with me to stay, and for a day or two everything would be fine, and then, of course, it would all start again. Nothing I did or said was ever right, and he made that quite clear to me.

By the spring of the following year things had disintegrated between us to such an extent that we were no longer sleeping together and he had embarked on an affair. When I discovered what was going on I confronted him one evening when he returned home from work.

'I know you are seeing someone,' I said quite calmly.

'What do you care?' he sneered back.

'I just want to know, that's all. I want to know what's going on between us.'

'Nothing is going on between us, you've seen to that!'

Bronner had reached boiling point and was now shouting at the top of his voice.

'So I'm sleeping with someone – so what?' He was taunting me and I couldn't take it any more. I ran out of the kitchen in tears and seconds later I heard the door slam.

Bronner had left.

I sobbed for what felt like hours. My marriage was in crisis and I couldn't see any way to make things better. Eventually I pulled myself together. I wanted some company and a shoulder to cry on so I called a friend who had become a great support and asked him to come round for a chat.

The events of that evening have stayed with me in perfect detail. He arrived and we shared a bottle of wine and talked. I was teary but calm and I felt it was really helping to talk things through honestly. I didn't realise it had got late and Bronner still wasn't back but I wasn't that surprised. I figured he'd gone round to his girlfriend's. I wanted to go to bed; I was exhausted. When I asked my friend to go, though, he looked surprised. He made it clear that he'd imagined I planned to get over the collapse of my marriage by having sex with him. Nothing could have been further from the truth and I told him so. His mood changed. The considerate man I liked became insistent. He tried to kiss me, put his arms around me. I asked him to stop and when he didn't I pushed him away. By now I was actually frightened, I couldn't quite believe what was happening. But he didn't stop and now he was angry.

He fell to the floor on top of me. I tried again to push him away but it was no use. I was helpless under his weight. With his left hand he pinned my arms above my head and with his other he pushed up my skirt, and started tugging at my underwear. I begged him to stop but he wouldn't listen. Instead he tore my knickers to the side so forcibly that they cut into me. And with that he raped me.

When he had finished he got up, leaving me on the floor, sobbing. Without a second glance he made his way over to the table, picked up his keys and coat from a chair and walked out of the flat, slamming the door behind him.

I couldn't believe what had happened. I tried to lift myself from the floor but I was in so much pain that it was a struggle. When I gathered enough strength to get to my knees, I looked down to see blood trickling down my thighs.

Somehow I managed to make it into the bedroom and slumped on to the bed. Daisy was still asleep and Bronner was still out. I was in a state of shock and I didn't know what to do. I lay down and tried to rest, but it was no use, I was in too much pain to sleep. By the morning I was in such agony that I knew I had to get some help, so I called my mother. She came to the flat immediately and when she saw the state I was in she telephoned a doctor.

The attack had been so brutal and vicious that I was admitted to the Cromwell Hospital, where I remained for a week. I was put on a course of morphine to take the pain away and had to be given sixteen internal stitches. On top of this I had to be given antibiotics, because he had infected me. Mr O'Sullivan, the consultant gynaecologist who treated me, was so alarmed by the extent of my injuries that he urged me to press charges, offering to testify as a witness if I did. I didn't. I just couldn't face it. I was traumatised, I felt utterly wretched, and all I could think about was getting home to Daisy as soon as possible.

When Gavin and Zoë visited me the next day they were so shocked by the sight of me lying in that hospital bed, bruised and delirious from the morphine, that they were unable to speak for the first few minutes. 'I cannot believe he did this,' Gavin said. 'You should report him.' I knew he was right but I still couldn't bear the thought of the process. I said I would think about it but I knew my mind was made up.

On my return from the hospital Bronner was at the flat. He hadn't rallied round after the attack. We hadn't been brought closer together, and I couldn't help feeling that the rape had happened partly because I was in such a vulnerable position after our fight. I had been desperate before but this made me lower than ever. It was the crisis that made us both realise that the relationship was over, and shortly afterwards we broke up. A week after my 22nd birthday Bronner announced that he was off to live with the girl he had been having an affair with. To be honest, it was a huge relief to me. Although I was scared of what lay ahead, frightened of being on my own, I knew that I couldn't go on like this. My family and friends were thrilled when I told them he had left. Of course, none of them wanted to see me hurt or alone, but they knew that even though I was in a desperate state, I was better off without him.

When I first told Bronner that I was pregnant he had promised to support our child whatever happened between the two of us, but after he left me we received nothing. Friends urged me to seek child support from him through the courts, but I wasn't having any of it. If he didn't want to support his child of his own accord, then I didn't want anything from him. I would take care of Daisy myself. Of course, this could and should have been the moment when I denied him access to Daisy, but I was determined that my daughter shouldn't be denied a relationship with her father, even if he wasn't willing to support her financially.

Bronner's contact with Daisy was sporadic. He would come by from time to time, when it suited him, to see her. He never brought her anything, never asked how I was coping, but then that was Bronner through and through. I put up with it for the sake of my child and granted him whatever access he wanted. We kept this up for over a year until one day in the spring of 1991 I decided to cut ties with Bronner altogether. During a visit to his flat in Maida Vale, Daisy, who had only just celebrated her second birthday, wet herself whilst sitting on his knee. It was a simple accident that could have happened to any child, and one that any adult, in their right mind, should have laughed off. But Bronner didn't laugh it off. Instead he took his hand to her. Like most parents I am of the opinion that there is a great difference between giving a child a light smack on the bottom and actually hitting them, and unfortunately this fell into the latter category. I'm not saying that he hit her hard, but it was certainly forceful enough for her to cry out and for her to remember the incident to this day.

After that I stopped him from seeing her altogether. If he wasn't going to treat his daughter properly, with the love, care and compassion she deserved, then there was no point in us maintaining this charade any longer. I refused to have anything more to do with Bronner. My parents tried to maintain a relationship with his mother and father, and on a couple of occasions they even took Daisy out to stay with them in America so she could get to know her family, but as far as I was concerned I wanted nothing more to do with this man.

Although I was determined to raise Daisy by myself, the whole notion of single parenthood filled me with terror. In those first few months after Bronner left I would lie awake at night wondering how we were going to survive. With the money I got from the state I knew we could get by, but I certainly didn't have the funds to provide for my child in the way that I wanted, and I knew this was going to get increasingly difficult as she grew up. I was so in love with Daisy by now that the thought of her having to go without anything filled me with a sense of despair. She wouldn't go hungry, but she wouldn't have the childhood that I'd had. And it was then

47

that I realised just how lucky I had been, and for the first time in my life I really started to appreciate my parents. I began to see just how hard they had worked, and how much they had sacrificed, to give us an idyllic childhood. And it was then, also for the first time, that I understood just how badly I had treated them. I suppose, looking back, I did a lot of growing up during that period.

I certainly couldn't have survived without the support of my parents in the aftermath of the rape. They helped with practicalities and childcare but, more importantly, they enabled me to heal. A massive part of me simply wanted to forget about what had happened and thanks to my parents, Daisy, Zoë and Gavin, I felt loved and protected. With Bronner gone, I felt I had a chance to fight back, against the sense of vulnerability and horror that had been plaguing me. I wanted to resist the despair I had felt in the first few days and weeks after the attack and I hoped I was strong enough to do it. For a little while, I thought I was.

5

Lost In Music

In the weeks after Bronner left, my parents did everything they could to help me out financially, but I realised that I couldn't go on relying on their handouts for ever. My father had lost a lot of money during the late 1980s as a result of the stockmarket crash, and I was well aware of the fact that they were struggling themselves. I knew that I was going to have to get some work, and for a time took modelling jobs where and when I could, but I found it hard to juggle motherhood with last-minute castings and shoots that went on well into the night, and in any case that kind of work didn't provide a regular income. As the months went on I became increasingly concerned about our future and determined to find a career, so I could take care of my child myself. If having a baby had given me anything it was a sense of purpose in my life. I realised that I no longer wanted to drift from job to job until I got bored, or to work simply to make ends meet. I wanted to make something out of my life. There was a part of me, still struggling with the aftermath of the rape, that needed to prove that I could be someone – someone my daughter could be proud of – and I knew who that someone was, for deep in my heart I had always known what I wanted to be. I wanted to be a singer.

From an early age music had always been my great passion. When I was a small child I loved it when my parents played records or put the radio on, and by the time I hit my teens and owned a stereo of my own I would spend hours locked in my bedroom listening to music. But unlike other girls of my age I wasn't interested in what was popular in the charts at the time; my tastes were far more eclectic, thanks in part to my elder brothers, who prided themselves on their musical knowledge. I would raid their collections when they were out and would sit listening to their records and tapes. By my early teens I was listening to the likes of David Bowie, Fleetwood Mac and the Jam. I liked the moody sounds of Nina Simone and Billie Holiday. I was a great fan of Stevie Nicks and, in her incarnation as Blondie, I loved Debbie Harry, as much for her look and punky, strong attitude as for her voice. I would lie on my bed listening to these artists and would dream of one day making it as a professional singer.

It was an ambition I know many young girls share. What could be more exciting, after all, than standing on stage in front of a stadium full of fans, all screaming out your name? What could be better than making it as a big recording star and enjoying all the frills and trappings that went with the job? But in fact I wasn't interested in any of that. I didn't want to be famous for the sake of it. I didn't harbour any ambitions to be rich. I didn't really want the attention. For me it was all about making music and being able to perform it. I didn't want to be a commercial artist; what I wanted was to be a respected talent; and, even at that young age, I recognised the difference between the two. I'd have been quite happy to perform the music I loved and had written myself in a small, smoky jazz club rather than to appear on *Top of the Pops* singing some manufactured hit. I just wanted to do my own thing.

I kept these thoughts quite secret from my family and friends when I was a young teenager, fearing they would laugh at me for having such precocious ideas about my future and career. But that didn't stop me from dreaming that one day I would make it, and it didn't stop me from trying. I would sit in my room after school, when my parents thought I was busy doing my homework, writing songs. Pages and pages of lyrics, most of them reflecting my mood at the time, which was obviously quite dark, as I was a teenager – and, as such, embarrassing to look back on now. When my mother discovered a stack of these lyrics hidden amongst my possessions when she was clearing up my room one day, she was horrified. She claimed that she never set out to read them, but when the words 'suicide', 'death', 'darkness' and 'pain' in my teenage scrawl screamed out at her from a single sheet of A4 paper, she felt, like any concerned parent, that she had no choice but to go through them. When I got home from school that afternoon she sat me down and gently asked if anything was 'wrong' or whether I needed to 'see' someone.

'No, I don't!' I shouted, furious that she had been rifling through my things. 'There is nothing "wrong" with me – but there is with you. How dare you go through my things? That was private! And you should know better than to read people's personal thoughts!'

'So there isn't anything you want to tell me?' she asked tentatively.

'No!'

'But these thoughts you have . . . these things you are writing about in your poems . . . what's it all about?'

'They aren't poems, they are lyrics! It's music! Just music!' And with that I slammed the kitchen door and went back to my room to write some more angry verses.

In truth the dark thoughts and moods I was experiencing came down to nothing more than teenage angst, for my life really couldn't have been happier or more comfortable back then. Now that I was battling with some much more serious demons, I saw music as a refuge as well as a job.

Music was very much in my blood. My maternal grandmother had been a saxophonist and violinist and in the 1930s was part of an all-girl band that travelled across Britain and Europe performing alongside jazz legends such as Benny Goodman. She was very much ahead of her time, bobbing her hair long before it was fashionable, and dressing in a way that was deemed 'innovative' for that particular era.

Although I never knew my grandmother, I always felt spiritually connected to her, something I have always believed had to do with the fact that she died on the day I was born. When my grandmother heard the news that my mother had given birth to a baby girl she travelled the whole way from Bournemouth to London to visit her at the hospital and meet her grandchild for the first time. My mother recalls how she held me in her arms that day and welcomed me into the world. She was delighted that my mother had given birth to a girl, knowing that she had desperately wanted a daughter to complete her family. But on the train back home, tragedy struck. My grandmother suffered a fatal heart attack. My mother was, of course, distraught. What should have been one of the happiest days of her life suddenly turned into the saddest. They had always enjoyed an extremely close relationship, and so my grandmother's sudden death came as a huge blow to my mother. In some way she felt responsible, convincing herself that it was her fault that my grandmother had died, and she bore this guilt for many years. Before I was born my parents wanted to call me Rachel, but after this tragedy they decided that it was fitting to name me after my grandmother, and so I was given her first name, Pearl. In fact for many years my mother found it too distressing to call me that, and during my early childhood I was known to family and friends as Sam – an abbreviation of my second name, Samantha. It wasn't until my early teens that my mother was finally able to bring herself to call me Pearl and I started using the name.

I knew the day I left school that I wanted to make it as a singer, but I just didn't know where to begin. My parents and friends didn't know anyone in that world, I had no contacts, and I wasn't sure how you broke into the industry. They certainly didn't offer career advice at school about becoming a recording artist. When I tried modelling and took acting classes, it wasn't because I thought I was especially pretty or wanted to be a star, I simply figured that those worlds might somehow offer a gateway into the music business, but neither profession offered me the break I so desperately craved.

Whilst I was with Bronner I could never have pursued my dream. I simply didn't have the energy or the self-confidence, and I also had a young baby to care for, but now that he had gone and Daisy was older, things were different for me. Although I had stopped relying on my parents for financial support, they were still helping me in so many other ways. After everything that had happened, they were both determined that I should be able to rebuild my life in some way. In the first few months after the attack and Bronner leaving I wasn't interested in going out. I had reached my lowest ebb and had no desire to do anything or go anywhere. I just wanted to be at home with my daughter.

'You have to try and get your life back together,' my mother told me. 'You're young and you can start again. You must get out there, see your friends, find something that you want to do in life. I know that Daisy is your number one priority and that you don't have any support, but your father and I are here for you. We'll do anything we can to help.'

And they did. They created a second home for Daisy and encouraged me to let them have her for the night when I was going out. If I was working or had an appointment, they would collect her from nursery and would have her for the day, and whenever they went away on holiday they took her with them. After a few months, I began to feel better and more optimistic about my future.

I made a lot of changes during that time. I moved out of my basement flat in Shirland Road and ended up moving into a beautiful apartment in Primrose Hill with Zoë. Owned by my friend the photographer and video director Jamie Morgan, the flat looked like a miniature Manhattan loft and I fell in love with it the moment I walked through the door. When Jamie asked us whether we would like to house-sit for him while he went to America I couldn't believe my luck. I had so many bad memories of Shirland Road and I knew that the move would do me good. We were only supposed to stay there for six months, but I ended up staying for four years. Living with Zoë meant I had adult company and made me feel safer. Living alone would have been difficult because I was so conscious of potential danger lurking everywhere, but thanks to my parents' help with Daisy and Zoë's help in overcoming my fears, I could now go out at night to dinner, the cinema or even a nightclub, without worrying about the cost of a baby-sitter, and I was also able to work. I took modelling jobs whenever they came my way and was able to make ends meet. I still wanted to make a career for myself as a singer, but I knew that for the moment I would have to put that plan on the back burner. I needed a bit more time to get my confidence back before I took the plunge. I was terrified of rejection and struggling to rebuild my trust in the world, and in men.

Instead I took a job waiting tables at a club in London called 41 Beak Street. It may not have been the most glamorous work in the world, but it suited me fine because the club, situated in the heart of Soho, was a famous music industry haunt. Its bar and restaurant were frequented by industry executives as well as artists such as Neneh Cherry and the DJ and producer Nellee Hooper. When I wasn't serving dinner and drinks to the likes of these people I'd sidle up to them and ask for advice about how to get my career off the ground. No one seemed to mind – they were used to it. Everyone who worked the floor at Beak Street seemed to want to break into the business. 'Get a demo tape together' was their usual response. The only one who did mind, it seemed, was the manager, and I was frequently threatened with the sack when he caught me in the act. But aside from rubbing shoulders with these people there were other perks to the job. Though the initial pay wasn't great, I soon learnt that I could triple my earnings in a night from the tips alone. All the customers had such a good time that they thought nothing of slipping you a couple of ten-pound notes on top of their bill.

This, combined with having eaten for free – by feasting, scavenger-like, on the leftovers on their plates on the way down to the kitchen – meant that I would have enough money to pay for a baby-sitter. It was an enormous relief to me, because I could now work at night when Daisy was asleep and afford to spend the days with her when she was up and about.

I had been at Beak Street for over a year when I finally got my first break. I had a night off from work and was at a club called Subterranea, in Notting Hill, with a group of girlfriends when a man came up to me at the bar and introduced himself. He handed me his card, explaining that he was a talent spotter and that he had been watching me on the dance floor. For a moment I thought he must be spinning me a line, trying to chat me up, but he appeared quite genuine, his card seemed authentic, and he didn't look like a pervert.

'How would you like to come and work on a music project I'm involved with?' he asked.

'What?' The music was so loud that it was a struggle to hear what he was saying.

'A music video. We're scouting for singers and dancers for it and I think you'd be perfect.'

'But you haven't heard me sing!'

'No, but I've seen you dance and in any case it doesn't matter. You've got a sexy voice and you look the part, so how about it?'

I wasn't sure what to say but, egged on by my friends, I eventually accepted the offer. I turned up to a studio in Swiss Cottage the following week and we got to work. They sampled my voice and, to my surprise, liked what they heard so much that they used my vocals on the track. I don't know what happened to the single after that, whether it was ever released or not, but what I do know is that the experience gave me a new-found confidence and belief in myself. I couldn't really believe how lucky I had been. So it wasn't the 'big' break I had fantasised about for so long – but it was still a break.

'I think I could really make a go of it,' I told Gavin afterwards.

'Well, if that's what you want to do, then you should have a go. If you don't try, then you will never know. But you'll have to work on that voice of yours,' he laughed.

'I know that, so I'm thinking of taking singing lessons.'

'You are?'

'Yes, why not? I want to give this my best shot.'

'That's great,' he said. 'But you know it's not all about voice, Pearl. You need some material, some songs and you need a band.'

'Will you help me?'

'Of course.'

Gavin kept his word. He was so relieved to see me taking an interest in life and putting my troubles behind me. He had been a huge support and now we set about writing some songs together. I formed a band with Zoë and made a demo tape. With a small advance from Sony Music, who were keen to support new talent at the time, we were able to hire a studio for the day and we laid down a couple of tracks. We sent the tapes off to record companies and the response was on the whole quite favourable. However, much as I loved Zoë and liked working alongside her, I decided not to continue with our band. I wanted to go it alone and do this for myself, because I had a very definite view of the direction I wanted to take with my music and I was aware that this could jeopardise our friendship. Of course, I still needed to work with a band, but I wanted to put my own together. In the meantime, to gain some experience of singing live, I put an ad in the *NME*, offering my services as a singer, and it wasn't long before the phone started to ring. I worked with a number of up-and-coming bands during that time, playing gigs at pubs and small clubs around London.

During the day, whilst Daisy was at nursery, I went to singing lessons, auditions and rehearsals and met up with contacts within the industry. At night, when she was tucked up in bed, I'd work on new material. I took it all very seriously and tried to learn as much, I could over the next year, but it wasn't until 1993 that my career really started to get off the ground.

An A&R man from Island Consultancy, who had seen me perform at a gig, suggested that I should meet up with a musician called Owen Vyse. He thought that we would work well together and that Owen could help me with my material. I had never met Owen, but I knew who he was. He was a singer and guitarist with a band called Starclub, who were tipped to be the next big band on the scene. Thrilled that someone with his talent should want to work with me, I readily agreed to a meeting, and a week later Owen turned up at the flat. In the end we never did collaborate together, but we did start seeing each other. Owen was my first relationship since the attack and my break-up with Bronner. He was calm and sensitive and, above all, deeply caring. He enabled me to trust him and he treated me with the utmost sensitivity. He was also extremely creative and passionate about music. He was a brilliant guitarist and had a beautiful voice. We'd sit in my flat for hours talking about music and playing records, and we'd go to gigs to watch other bands play. Owen didn't particularly rate my voice, but he never knocked my ambition; if anything he nurtured it. He could see that I had potential, that there was a package there.

'What you really need to do is get your own band together,' he said to me one evening after he'd come to watch me perform at a gig. 'I think it's great what you're doing, but you can do better than that. You could really go somewhere.'

'You really think so?'

'Yes I do, but the key is finding the right people for your band, people who have the same musical direction as you.'

'How do I find them?'

'Put an advert in the music press and start auditioning.'

Taking Owen's advice, I set a date for the audition, advertised it in the *NME* and *Melody Maker* and hired a rehearsal room. Within a fortnight I had put together my perfect band. On guitar was Mark Thomas, who was also a gifted songwriter, on bass was Tim McTighe, and on drums we had a great young guy called James. As far as I was concerned I had found my dream team, so all I had to do now was to come up with a name for us. I chose Powder.

Once Mark and I had worked on some material for the band, we set about trying to get ourselves some bookings, with the help of our manager Tony Beard. For a time we just played small venues, but that was fine with us because we knew we needed both the practice and the experience. It paid off, for after a couple of months of hard graft we came to the attention of John Best and Phil Savidge, two of the biggest names in music PR. They took us on, and before we knew it they were getting us proper bookings.

Our first major gig was held at the Monarch, on the Chalk Farm Road. For us it was a huge deal to play the Monarch for it was there that so many bands of that era first cut their teeth. Having only ever performed in pubs and small music clubs at that stage, I remember being incredibly nervous when I first went out on stage, but the crowd that night gave us a warm reception and we even managed to get a mention in the music press the following week. We went on to play the Dublin Castle, in Camden, and following the gig we received our first serious accolade – a favourable review in the *NME*. By the time we performed at the Monarch for a second time there was quite a buzz surrounding us. Crowds of people queued up to see us that night, and when I came off stage I was told that Mick Jones from the Clash, Damon Albarn from Blur and Jarvis Cocker and Steve Makey from Pulp were in the audience. I couldn't really believe it. After the gig I was introduced to Steve, who congratulated me on my performance.

'What are you doing now?' he asked.

'I've got no idea,' I replied.

'Well, we are all going back to my house. Why don't you guys come along?'

'Are you sure that's OK?'

'Of course. Let's go.'

I had always hoped that as a band we would do well and achieve a modicum of respect from people within the industry, but I hadn't prepared myself for this. Not only were we hanging out with the likes of Pulp and getting recognition from the music press, but in just a matter of weeks we secured a £100,000 publishing deal from Island Polygram Publications and our first single, '20th Century Gods', went straight to the top of the indie charts.

Although thrilled by our success, I quickly learnt that if we were going to stay up there then we were going to have to work hard. The fact that we had made waves in the industry didn't mean that our future was by any means secure. Bands came and went the whole time – that was just the nature of the game we were in. If we were going to make it big, then we would have to put a lot more into it, and work on our songs, our act and our image.

'For one thing you're going to have to start lying about your age,' I was told by Parkway during our first meeting.

'But I'm only 25!'

'You may think that you're still young at *only* 25, but in this industry that's a bit long in the tooth, especially for a girl. We think you should shave two years off your age at least. From now on, as far as anyone is concerned, you are 23.'

I wasn't exactly comfortable with the idea of lying about my age, but what could I do? I didn't want to blow this opportunity and ruin everything for the rest of the band by not playing ball, and so even though it went against all my principles I did what I was told.

Although my parents had never really understood my music, they had always supported me in what I had wanted to do. It was quite obvious that I was never going to follow the conventional route in life and settle for a nine to five existence. They knew that what I wanted more than anything was to sing and that, aside from Daisy, music was my one great love. Of course, like any parent of a creative child, they had their reservations about my chosen career path. They knew that the industry was fiercely competitive and fickle, and they worried about how I would cope with the rejection if it didn't work out for me. But over the past few years my parents had also seen me work hard for my dream, whether it had been waiting on tables, writing music or putting in time with the band, so when it finally became a reality and we were taken on by Parkway, they were adamant that now I had been given this chance I should make the most of it.

It was they who came up with the suggestion that Daisy should come and live with them for half of the week, as well as on those nights when I was either on tour or performing. They would set up a proper bedroom for her, creating a home from home, so there would be some continuity and stability to her upbringing. Of course, I didn't want to be parted from Daisy at all. I found one night away from her hard enough as it was, but I could see their point. Most weeks I was already spending two to three nights away from her, performing with the band, and I was well aware that as our success and reputation grew these absences would become all the more frequent. I had childcare and now could afford all the baby-sitters I wanted, but I knew that for Daisy this wasn't the same as being with her family. At least this way I could see Daisy every day when I was in London and wasn't working, as my parents lived round the corner from me. I also had the reassuring knowledge that she was with people she loved and who loved her back, instead of being left with a complete stranger for the night. It wasn't an easy decision for me to make, but I knew that if I was going to give my music career any chance at all it was the most sensible one.

Owen was pleased by our success and was a great support

to me during this time. I owed a lot to him, for had it not been for him I very much doubt that I would have got anywhere. And of course he'd helped me to deal with some very dark feelings. But, grateful as I was, and much as I loved him, I knew by the end of the year that our relationship had stalled. Because of our careers we spent less and less time together, and eventually we came to the mutual and amicable decision to go our separate ways. Fortunately, I had enough friends to get me through the break-up. Not only did I have Gavin and Zoë around me, but I had made friends within the industry as well. Steve Makey and I had become incredibly close. I'd introduced him to Zoë and they had started seeing each other, so we spent a lot of time hanging out together with Jarvis Cocker. I was great friends with the members of a group called Menswear and got on well with the girls from Elastica. And I also had my band, who had become like a second family to me as we spent so much time together either on the road or in the studio.

By the beginning of 1995 Powder were doing well and we had made a name for ourselves. We were getting a lot of press, had a good fan base and were producing some great material. On top of this we had just been asked to support Elastica on tour, which was a great honour for us as they were one of the biggest bands on the scene at the time. We travelled the country doing gig after gig, and were also signed up to perform in some of the festivals that summer, including Reading. It was an unbelievably exciting time for us as a band, as well as for me personally. I had always dreamt of making it in the music industry, and now that dream was my reality.

6

High Times

I had always been acutely aware that if Powder were going to last the distance then we were going to have to work hard and put one hundred per cent into everything we did. I had enough friends within the industry to know that it wasn't just a case of turning up to a gig or a recording studio and belting out a couple of tunes; there was a lot more to it than that. And it wasn't enough to just to get your break; you had to make your mark. As well as playing the established London venues you had to be prepared to get on the road and take your music across the country, performing at gigs in pubs and clubs, no matter how small, squalid or empty they were. In our first year as a band we seemed to spend more hours on motorways in tour buses than we ever did playing together.

On top of this we had press to do. There were countless interviews and shoots with the music publications, and if you were lucky enough to have the right exposure then there were radio and television appearances to turn up for. We also had to think about our image, for that was, in many ways, just as important as what we sounded like. Although this wasn't so crucial for the boys, it was essential that I, as the lead singer, looked the part. I spent endless hours working on my clothes, hair and make-up, because I was well aware that my look should complement the direction of the band. I also wanted to stand out from all the other girls on the indie scene, which meant not conforming to the standard uniform of jeans, T-shirts and Doc Martins. Instead I opted for heels and vintage dresses, bobbed my hair in the style of the silent movie star Louise Brooks, kohled my eyes and rouged my cheeks and lips. I remember Justine Frischmann from Elastica taking me aside one day and advising me not to wear dresses as she thought that it would alienate my girl fan base, but I disagreed. I believed that dressing like a girl rather than a man would only appeal to them more. From the outset I knew that we had to sell ourselves to the public and the press, and that if we were going to make it in this industry then we had to be as much of a brand as we were a band. Making music was just a small part of what we did, but I didn't mind. At that stage I was so ambitious for Powder to do well that I was more than prepared for the hard graft.

But it wasn't all work, for this was an industry where people partied as hard as they played. There were the festivals, the tours, the industry shindigs, the impromptu get-togethers back at people's flats, houses or hotel rooms, the awards ceremonies, the after-show parties. Even a late-night recording session at a studio could turn into a party provided you had the right combination of people and enough alcohol. And then, of course, there were the drugs.

In the mid-1990s when the Britpop movement was in full swing, indulging in illicit substances was very much a part of the culture. To be rock and roll, to have that edge, it was almost a prerequisite to take drugs, and hardly anyone within the industry frowned upon it. If a band was playing at a gig or a festival it was completely acceptable for then to ask their management to score some gear for them. To celebrate signing a new record deal, as well as opening a bottle of champagne your A&R man would be offering you a line of cocaine. You would take drugs to get the creative juices flowing when you were writing, you'd use them to get you through a late-night recording session, you would rely on them to help you unwind after a performance.

It wasn't just the artists and musicians who used. From the studio bosses to the press officers, from the producers to the roadies, back in those days everyone seemed to be doing drugs. I remember at the beginning of my career giving an interview to quite an established music journalist who was so high on cocaine during our hour together that not only did his nose run throughout, but he spent most of the session jabbering on about himself rather than asking us about our music. As a result he was forced to make up most of what we said when he came to write up the piece, liberally misquoting what we'd said about other bands on the scene at the time. This was unfortunate, to say the least, when we had to deal with some of those bands mentioned in the article.

I was, of course, no stranger to the world of drugs, having used quite openly and regularly during my teens. but the moment I discovered I was carrying Daisy I had turned my back on that life and for a good couple of years had abstained from all mind-altering substances, with the exception of the odd joint or two to help me relax. I was a devoted mother. I didn't want to be out of it. I had responsibilities and it just wasn't right to be indulging in drugs. But now that Daisy wasn't with me round the clock I had the freedom to party and less of an incentive to stay clean, and so when someone offered me drugs it was all too tempting just to say yes.

I suppose my problem was that I never really considered drugs to be dangerous. Sure, I had sat and yawned through enough lectures at school to know better, and I'd listened to my parents' and their friends' horror stories about the perils of drug addiction when I was growing up, but it never really struck a chord with me. I believed that it was just some kind of propaganda put out by a generation of people who couldn't possibly know what they were talking about because they had never experienced it themselves. To them all drugs were 'evil'. In their eyes there was no difference between smoking cannabis and taking smack. All drugs led down the road to ruin. But like so many of my contemporaries I didn't see it like that. The fact that you smoked a joint here or there or took a tab of ecstasy when you were out clubbing didn't necessarily mean that you would end up dead in a council estate having overdosed on smack. As far as I was concerned you were more likely to become addicted to alcohol – a legal, socially acceptable, readily available drug that you could purchase over the counter – than you were to an illicit substance you had to go out of your way to find. As long as you were careful, and you were in control, then drugs were nothing more than a bit of fun, a way of escaping for an hour or two. And I was always careful, always in control. I hadn't used them when I was pregnant with Daisy or when she was in my care, but then I hadn't smoked cigarettes or drunk alcohol either. It was all about being a responsible mother and putting her health and welfare first. It wasn't about the drugs themselves.

So in the early days of Powder I didn't think twice about using drugs when I was away from Daisy and would happily 'dabble' in them with my peers. I'd pop a couple of ecstasy pills if we were out clubbing, take a line of coke at a late-night party or if I wanted to stay up after a gig, smoke some weed with my band mates, drop an acid tab if I wanted to have a laugh. But by most of my contemporaries' standards at that stage my drug use was mild. Because it didn't take a lot for me to get quite out of it, the actual amount of drugs I took was always fairly small. If we went to a party, it would take just one line of coke to get me going; if I went to a club, just two tabs of ecstasy was all that I needed to stay on the dance floor till dawn. To those who have never taken drugs that might seem like a vast amount, but at that time, within the world that I moved in, it was measured. I was hanging out with people who would happily tuck into a gram of coke a night or would take four to five tabs of ecstasy when they were partying. By their standards I was a mere novice.

Although I was happy to indulge when I was offered drugs, I would say my use was purely recreational at this stage. I knew that I wasn't dependent on them. There were times, of course, when I used a couple of days in a row, especially if I was on the road touring. I would smoke joints in our bus to relieve the boredom on the way to a gig, maybe indulge in a line of coke if I was offered it afterwards, take ecstasy the following day if I went to a party, and then use marijuana again to help with the come-down. But for every time this happened there would be weeks when I didn't use at all, especially if I was seeing or caring for Daisy. I liked to keep those two parts of my life completely separate, and I was determined that she should never see me hung over or, God forbid, out of it. And I didn't mind these times. I could happily operate without drugs if I wanted to. If they weren't around I didn't give it a second thought.

When it came to using drugs back then it wasn't really a question of me wanting to get high, it was really about fitting in. I wanted to be part of the scene, in fact I desperately craved to be accepted, so saying yes to a joint, a small line of cocaine, a tab of ecstasy or acid seemed like an easy ticket into the party. Sharing drugs with your friends put you on a level with them. I didn't want to be the girl who went home early, the party pooper, the one who said 'no'. I wanted to be in the thick of it. It seemed churlish not to have a line of coke if it was offered to you at a party by some industry bigwig, boring to be the only one not coming up on an E at a club, lonely to be the one person in the room not getting the joke because you weren't stoned. I took drugs because other people did. Looking back now, I can see that it was my inability to stop following the crowd that would ultimately lead to my downfall.

Because I was able to take and leave drugs when I wanted, it never occurred to me that I could ever become addicted to them. My desire for the high they gave me simply wasn't strong enough. Yes, I got a kick from cocaine, but it always made me feel slightly edgy once the initial buzz had worn off. I enjoyed the way ecstasy made me feel on the night, high on the joys of life and love, but the come-down from it was invariably so bad that in hindsight I often wondered whether it was really worth it. The occasional tab of acid could be fun, but I was always slightly mindful of and apprehensive about where each trip would take me. There was only one substance

I felt completely comfortable using, and that was marijuana, but I never really considered that to be a drug at all. I simply couldn't ever see myself having a 'problem' with anything. Cigarettes, alcohol, dope, coke, uppers, downers, gambling, sex even – I just didn't see how people became addicted to such things. I knew I wouldn't, I couldn't, it just wasn't in my make-up. I was a strong enough personality and had enough will-power never to become dependent on anything. For a time that's what I honestly thought and believed – until I discovered heroin.

It was the mid-1990s and the boys and I had been booked to support one of the leading bands of the Britpop era on one leg of their UK tour. To save costs – ours not theirs – the band had allowed us to travel from London to the venue on their tour bus. It was a long journey, but no one seemed to care for we had come prepared. There were beers in the fridge, there was music on the stereo, and as we headed out of London up the motorway we were already in the party spirit. I was excited about the tour, not only because we had been booked to support such a major act, but because quite simply I had developed a crush on one of the band members. For months I had tried to get his attention, but he was not interested in me because he already had a girlfriend and he had made it quite clear to me for some time that we would never be anything more than friends. Nevertheless, this did little to quash my infatuation for him; if anything it just made my feelings all the more intense. In my hearts of hearts I knew that nothing would ever happen between us, but I still clung on to that strand of hope, and just to be in his immediate vicinity made my heart race like a schoolgirl's. So when he sauntered up the bus half-way through the journey and asked if I wanted a 'smoke' I was elated. As I was the only one on the bus not drinking, I was delighted that someone had some dope on them.

'Of course I would!' I said.

'Great,' he said, plonking himself down on the seat next to mine.

I had assumed that he would pull out some grass and some cigarette papers from his pocket, so I was slightly bemused when he started to fold some foil on the table in front of us. He took some resin from his jacket and placed it on the foil, which he was now holding in his hand, and lit it. When the resin had melted into a liquid he took another piece of foil, this time rolled into a tube, and inhaled the slightly rancid fumes. Once he had taken his hit he offered it to me.

Zoë, who had come with me for the ride and was sitting opposite me, shot me a look of alarm. She and I both knew what this was, and it wasn't dope. This was smack. Seeing Zoë's look of disproval and sensing my slight alarm, the guy laughed. 'Oh come on, girls! What is it with you?' he jeered gently. 'I thought you, Pearl, of all people would be up for it. We know how you like to party . . . Come on! Pearl?'

Zoë gestured that she didn't want any. I thought about refusing politely myself, but how could I? It was different for her, she was drinking, and in any case she didn't have the feelings I had for this man. She was in love, she had a boyfriend.

'You up for it, Pearl?' the guy asked again.

'OK . . .'

I was nervous about taking heroin. I didn't know how it was going to make me feel, and I had no idea how to do it, but all the preparations were gallantly made for me. Once the resin had melted I took my first hit, and within just a matter of minutes the fumes took hold of my system and my whole body and mind seemed to ascend into heaven. It was the most incredible thing I had ever taken. I had never felt quite so happy, so well or so carefree.

I didn't use heroin again for two years after that, but I knew from that first hit that I could easily become addicted to this drug: it had taken such a hold on me, made me feel so beautiful. I knew I had found my nirvana, but I also knew it was dangerous. I avoided heroin for as long as I could because I had the feeling that if I took it again, I might never be able to stop.

7

True Love

In finally achieving my dream and realising my ambitions in life I should have felt both happy and fulfilled. As a band we were doing well; we were receiving favourable reviews in the music press, making waves on the scene and getting recognition from the people that mattered in the business. At last I was making some decent money and could rest assured in the knowledge that I was able to provide for my daughter and her future. On the face of it I had everything going for me: the career I loved, a beautiful, healthy little girl, a lovely flat and a group of loyal friends. By the late summer of 1995, however, I was conscious that something was lacking in my life, and that feeling had started to cast a shadow over everything positive that was happening at the time.

The fact that I hadn't had the best of times in the preceding months didn't help matters. What should have been one of the most exciting summers of my life turned out to be a total washout. I was feeling quite vulnerable and lonely and I couldn't really cope with those feelings. I had, for example, planned to go to Glastonbury that year with all my friends, but by the time I got round to organising a ticket for myself it was completely sold out. I still hoped to cadge a lift with some of my music friends who were playing at the gig, but there wasn't room for me on the bus. So I was forced to watch the festival alone, at home, in front of the television.

It hadn't helped that I hadn't seen much of Zoë that summer either. Now that she was with Steve we spent a lot less time together, which was fair enough, but I did miss her. Gavin had hit the big time with his band Bush and was rarely in town any more. If he wasn't touring then he was in LA, where he had set up a second home. And if that wasn't bad enough, my parents had taken Daisy off to America for a holiday. I was delighted that she was going to have a proper break and appreciated the gesture my parents had made, but I hated being separated from her. We had become quite a team, Daisy and I, and I always felt lost when she wasn't around, as though a part of me was missing.

I felt quite alone in the world during that summer, and it was beginning to get to me. I was well aware of what I needed to fill the void in my life, and that was a boyfriend. I needed to be in a relationship with someone who both loved and respected me, but so far that had eluded me. It was very difficult trying to find someone I could trust after the rape and everything that had happened with Bronner, and I also had to factor Daisy into the equation. I couldn't just let anyone into my life these days. She was now old enough to form attachments with people, and I didn't want her to get hurt or disappointed if a relationship failed. I had to make sure that anyone I was with loved Daisy as much as they loved me, and since breaking up with Owen I hadn't met anyone who made the grade. Within the circle in which I moved there were few men ready to settle for what I had to offer. They may have wanted to date a singer, but were they prepared to take on someone with a six-year-old child? Over the last few months I had seen a couple of people, but I knew in my heart of hearts that none of them was right for me, and when I eventually did fall for someone in June that year, he suddenly announced, on our fourth date, that he had a girlfriend.

I had just about given up all hope of ever being happy again when suddenly my luck changed. I was lying in bed early one Saturday morning, listlessly watching children's TV after a restless night, when the phone rang.

'Pearl! Thank God you are in, I thought you might be away or still asleep . . .' It was a girlfriend of mine called Catherine. 'What are you up to?' she continued.

Fuck all, I thought, absolutely fuck all. I haven't been anywhere or seen anyone for weeks. I've just been lying here watching television like a zombie.

'Not much, what about you?'

'Well, I was hoping I could pop by. It's just I'm with Roger and we've been up all night at a party round the corner and now have nowhere to go, so I was wondering if we could come and hang out with you?'

Catherine and her friend Roger Sargent, the photographer, were at my front door within the hour, armed with bags filled to the brim with food for breakfast and bottles of wine.

'I hope you don't mind, but we brought some friends,' she said as she walked into the loft. With Catherine was another girlfriend and a man I had never met before called Andy Winters, who managed a group called Dodgy.

'The more the merrier,' I said, thankful to have some company at last.

A couple of hours later the party was in full swing. Catherine and I had got on the phone and asked everyone we knew who was at a loose end that day to come round. Zoë and Steve turned up with Jarvis in tow, and someone invited members of the Bluetones, one of the biggest indie bands on the scene then. By early afternoon there must have been at least twenty people crammed into my sitting-room. Now that everyone had gathered there was just one more call to make, and that was to a dealer. As I wasn't drinking, a couple of tabs of ecstasy and some grass would get me into the party spirit, and one of my guests knew of a guy who dealt locally.

In the middle of our revelries Andy asked if he could use the telephone. He was off to Belgium that night and needed to finalise his arrangements.

'Why are you going to Belgium?' I asked.

'The band are playing the Dour Festival.'

'Really? A festival!'

'Yeah, it's no big shakes but I have to go. To be honest I'd like to cancel, but I think I had better be there.'

A festival . . . I hadn't been to a festival all summer.

'Can I come?' I asked

'What?'

'Can I come along with you? I could really do with getting away for a night or two.'

Maybe it was the drugs talking, or maybe it was some kind of higher power – my spiritual guides, perhaps – but something inside me was telling me I had to go. I didn't care where this festival was, who was playing, who would be there or even how long it was going to take to get there, I just knew I had to be there and no one was going to dissuade me.

'Pearl, you really don't want to go there,' said Jarvis, always the voice of reason.

'Why not? It'll be fun!'

'You have to be kidding,' Steve piped up. 'Put it like this – it's not exactly Glastonbury or Reading. It's just a field in the middle of nowhere with a stage. Trust me, we've been there.'

'I don't care. I want to go,' I said, like a petulant child, ready to stamp her foot until she got her own way. 'Anything has got to be better than moping round here on my own all weekend.'

No one really expected me to go, and it seemed as if everyone in the room that afternoon was trying to talk me out of it, but I was on a mission, and so later that night I wound the party down and by one in the morning I was on the tour bus with Andy and his band, heading to Dover to catch the ferry to Calais. I was buzzing with excitement, as well as the third tab of ecstasy I had taken that evening. I couldn't believe that I was really going to Belgium. It all seemed so crazy, so spontaneous and fun, and I convinced myself that something magical was about to happen. Unfortunately, by the time we reached Dover and boarded the ferry, my enthusiasm had started to wane. The ecstasy was beginning to wear off and I was coming down. I tried to get some rest, spreading myself over a row of plastic chairs, but it was no use. I was blinded by the fluorescent lights of the ferry, it was too noisy to sleep, and to make matters worse I felt seasick. Suddenly, my great adventure didn't seem so great after all. What on earth am I doing, I kept thinking. Why am I chasing a party that just isn't going to happen? Why can't I just be happy with my lot? I should have stayed at home, called an end to the day like everyone else.

By the time the ferry docked in Calais and we had boarded the bus again, I started to feel slightly better. Dawn was breaking over the countryside as we crossed the border into Belgium, and by the time we reached the village of Dour, it had turned into the most beautiful, warm and sunny day. We checked into a hotel and, once we had got ourselves together, headed off towards the festival. Steve and Jarvis had been right, of course. This wasn't Reading, and it certainly wasn't Glastonbury. Compared to the festivals I had been to this was a glorified village fête, but I wasn't bothered. It was a lovely day and anything had to be better than sitting at home on my own.

As Andy and the band headed backstage to prepare for their set, I decided to get some rest and lay down on the grass, pulling my shades over my eyes. It was good to be outside, to feel the warmth of the sun on my face and listen to the bands warm up. After about an hour, feeling thirsty and in need of a bottle of water, I made my way to the hospitality tent. Having been to the bar I made my way to an empty table in the corner of the tent and sat down. And it was then that I noticed him. And he, in turn, noticed me.

He was sitting at a table just a couple of feet away from mine. He looked faintly familiar but I didn't know why. I couldn't place him, and I was sure that I hadn't met him before, but you couldn't forget a face like that. He appeared to be in the middle of an interview, for there was a woman at his table with a tape recorder and mike, but he didn't seem to be that engaged by what she was saying. Instead he kept looking in my direction. I tried not to catch his eye but I couldn't help it, because every time I looked up there he was, staring at me. I tried to hide behind my sunglasses but it was no use, he just kept staring. As the interview came to an end a man came up to him and had a word in his ear. I couldn't hear what they were saying, but at one point they both looked up at me and laughed. Feeling self-conscious, I quickly downed my bottle

of water and made my escape, seeking refuge in the ladies'
loo. When I came out he was there waiting for me.

'I'm Danny,' he said simply, putting out his hand. 'What's
your name?'

'Pearl.'

He nodded and smiled.

I don't know what it was about him, but from that very
first moment, those first words, I was completely captivated by
him. He wasn't like anyone I'd been attracted to before. In
the past I had always gone for older men, dark, edgy types,
slightly rough around the edges. And yet here was this young
boy, who couldn't have been more than 21 years old, standing
in front of me, chatting me up, and to my surprise I found
myself enjoying it. There was just something so appealing about
him. He was friendly, he was confident and he had a sense of
mischief to him. He had these large lips, so big they looked
almost swollen, and huge brown eyes, which twinkled every
time he smiled.

'What are you doing here?' he asked.

'I'm not sure really.'

'Are you on your own?'

'No, well, yes, kind of. I came out with a band, but I'm not
with them. They are backstage at the moment. What about you?'

'I'm with a band too. We're playing here today.'

'Which band are you with?'

'Supergrass,' he replied. And that's when I realised why he
looked familiar to me. I had seen Supergrass play before. The
first time I saw them was when Ian Astbury from the Cult took
me to one of their gigs at the Palais, in Hammersmith, and the
second time was on television, the weekend I missed Glastonbury.

I liked them a lot. There was just something so fresh and new about them with their quirky upbeat sound, and I knew that they were going to go far.

'Well, if you're on your own and not doing anything, how about you hang out with me for a while?' Danny said.

I wasn't sure how to react to this proposition. I didn't know this guy from Adam, but then again I didn't know anyone else at the festival. Why not while away some time with him? Who knows, it could be fun, I thought.

'OK . . .'

Danny smiled and took my hand and led me out of the tent.

'So, they tell me you are a nutter,' he said as we headed towards the crowds.

'Who told you that?'

Danny nodded in the direction of the man he had been talking to in the tent. 'My sound engineer, he saw me looking at you and tried to warn me off. Seems like you have quite a reputation.'

'That's so unfair! It's not true and I can't believe he said that to you!'

'Don't worry,' he said laughing. 'It didn't put me off . . .'

'Really?'

'On the contrary, it made me even more interested in you.'

Danny and I spent the rest of the day together. To shield us from the sun he constructed a makeshift Wendy house for us out of clothes and blankets, and we sat there all afternoon, in our own little tent, listening to the bands and talking. I was happy being in his company. He was warm, he was intelligent, he was easygoing and he had a sense of humour. One moment we would be having a heart to heart about something serious, the next we'd be in stitches on the grass laughing about the silliest thing. And it was then that the strangest thing happened to me: I realised that I loved him. Of course, it was pure madness. How could you love anyone after just a couple of hours? I didn't know him, he didn't know me, we were just two strangers having a good time. But even as I tried to quash these feelings for him, I couldn't help feeling that he was the one and that no one else would ever compare to him. These thoughts were running through my head when Danny suddenly turned to me and looked me straight in the eye. He took my hand, held it in his, leant forwards and kissed me.

From that moment onwards we didn't leave each other's side. When Danny was due on stage to perform with the band, he took me with him and let me watch from the side. Throughout their set he kept looking back at me, smiling and winking at me as he drummed away. Later that evening we scored some ecstasy and walked round the festival together hand in hand, stopping from time to time to kiss. By the time night fell we decided we'd had enough of the festival, and so we went back to my hotel.

We were as high as kites by the time we got there and just couldn't stop laughing. Back in my room Danny decided that we should have some fun and dress up. He rifled through my bag, pulled out some clothes and put them on and then raided my make-up bag. 'Let's play hairdressers!' he shouted, jumping up and down on the bed. I sat in the chair, doubled up with laughter. He held out his hand. 'Come on then, come here,' he said, pulling me on to the bed. 'Let's play!' he screamed. I had never, in my whole life, met anyone who had such an appetite for fun as Danny did. I had never met a man who would play ball with me like this, who liked to laugh, who liked to talk and above all who liked to listen. I knew that I could tell him anything. Even at the festival when I mentioned the fact that I had a six-year-old daughter he didn't baulk. He just sat there, took a sip of his drink, and said, 'That's so great. I love kids.' The look on his face was so genuine, so sincere, that I knew he meant it and wasn't just spinning me a line. I had finally met someone who was straight up, who was real and who told it as it was, and I admired him for that.

Once we tired of our hairdressing game we decided to have a bath together. I'm not sure why, it just seemed a good idea at the time. We lay there, talking, until the water went cold and then, when we were dry, we fell on to the bed, exhausted. That night we made love for the first time. Maybe it was quick, maybe we should have waited, but at the time it felt like the most natural thing in the world. The perfect ending to the most perfect day. And afterwards we fell asleep in each other's arms.

I really didn't want our time together to come to an end, but when we woke in the morning I had a sinking feeling that it was all over. When Danny realised what the time was he jumped out of bed and pulled on his clothes.

'Shit! I've got to go!'

'Go where?' I murmured from under the bedclothes.

'I've got to make the morning ferry home with the band. We're off on tour this week and there's a lot to do. What time are you off?'

'I don't know,' I replied. 'I think we're going on the afternoon ferry.'

'Oh good,' he said, searching for his shoes. I could tell he wasn't really paying attention to what I was saying. Oh God, this is it, I thought. I'm never going to see Danny again. It was just a one-night stand, just a festival fling. How stupid I was to think that anything could ever come of it.

I was still lying in bed when he came over and gave me a peck on the cheek.

'I guess I'll see you around . . .'

I was upset but was determined not to show it. If he was going to be so casual about what had happened between us, then fine, I'd play him at his own game.

'OK, see you,' I said, trying to sound as breezy as possible. And with that he picked up his things and left the room.

After an hour I got up, packed my bag and went to meet the others for the journey home. Everyone was completely jaded from the day before and no one felt like talking much on the bus, which suited me fine. When we got on to the ferry I left the others at the bar and made my way on to the top deck. I found a seat and sat there with a bag of cold, soggy chips on my lap, staring despondently out to sea. Why did this always happen to me? Why couldn't things ever work out the way I wanted them to? I berated myself for being so stupid. How could I have fallen for this guy? Why had I slept with him? He was only 23, he was in a band, he wasn't ready for a relationship, at least not with someone like me.

I was completely lost in thought when I felt a tap on my shoulder. 'You all right?' said a voice behind me.

I turned around and there he was, standing behind my seat, with that cheeky smile.

'You know, I'm really happy I ran into you,' he said, taking a seat next to me and reaching for a chip.

'You are?'

'Yes, I am. When we missed our ferry this morning I was actually quite pleased because I thought that I might end up on yours.'

'I thought you said you just wanted to see me "around"?' I said accusingly.

'Did I say that?'

'Yes, you did.'

He didn't say anything.

'Well, did you mean it or were you just joking around?'

He paused. 'I'll tell you what, why don't you come back to Oxford with me tonight? We can spend some time together before I go away.'

I was so confused I didn't know what to say. One minute he seemed to be giving me the brush-off, the next he was asking me home with him.

I was tempted to go back home with this crazy boy I had fallen completely head over heels for, but I knew that I couldn't and shouldn't. I had to get back to reality. I had things to do in London the following day and was due to meet up with the band for a studio session. I couldn't just leave them high and dry because I had developed an infatuation for some stranger.

'I can't. I want to, of course, but I just can't,' I told him. 'But I'll see you again, though, if that's what you want.'

'Of course that's what I want! So, come on, give it to me . . .'

'Give you what?'

'Give me your number then!'

8

Feel All Right

Danny called the next morning and asked if I was free that night. He was coming to London to do some press with his band mates and was hoping that we could get together in the evening. Although he had taken my number I hadn't really expected to hear from him before he left for the States, and I certainly hadn't bargained on seeing him, so I was thrilled by the call. We planned to meet up at the Astoria, in the West End, where I was going to watch a gig with some friends. I was so excited about our date that I couldn't keep my mind on anything all day. I found it difficult to concentrate during our studio session, and as soon as it had finished I hurried home to change. I arrived at the Astoria at 9 p.m. and cast my eye round the venue, but he wasn't there. An hour passed and then another, but there was still no sign of him. Neither of us owned a mobile phone at the time, so there was no way I could reach him When the gig came to an end at around 11 p.m. I gave up hope altogether. My initial feelings of disappointment and hurt turned to fury. How dare he stand me up? Who the hell did he think he was? No one treated me like this.

I was standing on the pavement saying goodbye to my friends when I heard a voice shout out my name. I turned round –

it was Danny, running up the street. 'I'm sorry! I'm so sorry . . .' he said, panting, when he got to where I was standing.

'This better be good,' I said gruffly.

'I'm sorry, I was at MTV doing an interview and I got stuck there. I tried to leave but I couldn't and I didn't know how to get hold of you. But I'm here now . . .'

I wanted to be cross with him, but I couldn't.

'Please forgive me. I've run all this way.'

I paused for a minute, wondering whether I should give him a piece of my mind just for good measure, but he looked so pitiful and cute that I just melted.

'OK, I forgive you.'

'Thank God for that!' he laughed. 'I'd hate to get on the wrong side of you! Now let's go for a drink; there's a bar I know round here that's open late . . .' He took me by the arm and we crossed the road.

'Fancy a line?' he whispered in my ear conspiratorially as we got to the bar door. 'I've got a gram on me.'

Danny and I spent the next three days together. He had been put up at the Cumberland Hotel, in Marble Arch, and insisted that I stayed there with him. I wasn't complaining. I had no intention of leaving his side. I wanted to spend as much time with him as possible before he left for America. The following day I accompanied him to the BBC's studios as he was due to perform on *Top of the Pops* that evening. I watched him rehearse with the band and stayed on for their performance. We went to a Marianne Faithfull concert together later that night, took ecstasy and spent the following day locked in our hotel room. It was a magical couple of days.

On our last night together we checked into a hotel near

I was about four when this was taken and my look hasn't changed –
patterned tights, bar shoes and a floral dress!

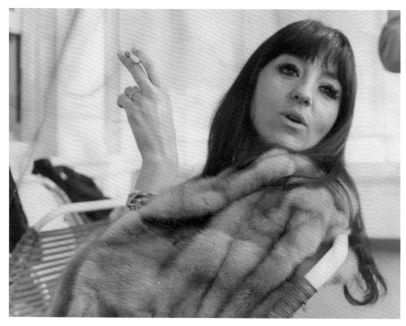

My glamorous mum.

Me and my dad . . .
I had a wonderful
childhood.

Me and my baby, Daisy.

I've been friends with
Zoë since I was 18.

Daisy was the best
thing that had ever
happened to me.

Gavin and I were
great friends. He
supported me
through some
awful times and
helped hugely
when I started
singing.

This was taken the night I met Danny. Looking at this picture, I'm surprised he fell for me!

Danny and I spent as much time together as we could.

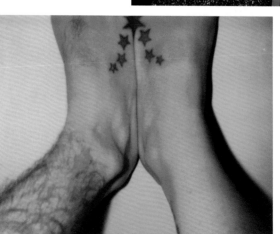

Four days after we met, we went to Brighton, took acid and got matching tattoos . . .

Backstage at a
Supergrass gig
in '95.

I was totally over the
moon when Powder
started to take off.
Being a singer was
my dream.

On our way to Reading Festival with Mark from Powder and his then girlfriend Faye.

Reading Festival '95. Our secret got out!

Oh dear!

On stage at the Monarch, the night we got discovered.

Rob, Mark, James and me. Having fun with some pillows!

Powder in the bath! This was taken on a really fun photo shoot,
even though it doesn't look it!

Gatwick airport. Danny's flight left early the next day, so it made sense to stay there. We both wanted to make the most of our time together and didn't want to spend our last night fretting about whether or not he would make his flight in the morning. Everything seemed to be going to plan. I drove us to the hotel, we checked in and went out for something to eat. We were getting on well, laughing and talking and making plans to see each other on his return to England, but when we got back to our room it suddenly all went horribly wrong. Danny and I had some grass on us and I rolled a joint for us to smoke before we went to bed, but the drug didn't have the desired effect on either of us. Rather than feeling happy and mellow and having a laugh together, we both became completely withdrawn. Up until then we had always been so comfortable in each other's company, so lively and talkative, but now we couldn't even communicate with one another. We sat there in silence for a while. When Danny did eventually speak, I completely misunderstood what he was saying. I was overwhelmed by paranoia by this stage and in my mind had decided that he hated me and was trying to tell me that it was over. In turn Danny believed that I was being cold towards him and was terrified that I was about to leave. I didn't, I stayed, but I had never felt so far apart from him before.

In the morning when we woke we tried to make amends, but there really wasn't time as Danny was in a hurry to get to the airport. As I dropped him off at the terminal he gave me a quick kiss and said that he would call me from the States, but as he walked into the departure lounge I was convinced that I would never see him again, that it was over. I drove back to London in tears.

Days passed and there was no word from him. I had barely moved from the flat since I got back from the airport, scared I might miss his call on my landline while I was out. By the weekend I still hadn't heard from him and resigned myself to the fact that if he had wanted to call me he would have done so by now and so I finally ventured out of the flat, away from the phone, and headed to a music festival with a friend. I hoped the excursion might act as a distraction from my sorrows, but in fact it just compounded them. Being at the festival just reminded me of him all the more, for I kept thinking back on our time together at Dour. Try as I might, I couldn't get Danny out of my head. I took a tab of acid hoping that would work but all it did was make matters worse. As the trip kicked in I began to hallucinate and all I could see was Danny's face everywhere. When we went to watch the Verve play on the main stage that evening, even Richard Ashcroft reminded me of him.

'I just don't get it,' I said to Gavin one day as we were taking one of our walks across Primrose Hill, with his dog Winston, a Hungarian Puli he had adopted from me shortly after I had Daisy. 'Why hasn't he called me, Gavin? Why? He took my number. He said he would call and he hasn't. What's that all about?'

'I don't know, darling,' he said. We found a patch of grass at the top of the hill and sat down. I pulled a joint from my pocket and lit up.

'How long has it been now?'

'A week, a whole week!'

'He will call, though, I'm sure of that,' he said.

'How can you be sure? He hasn't called so far.'

'Yes, but he will. He'd be a fool not to. Put it this way, you're gorgeous, you're sexy, you're successful and you know he likes you. The boy is going to call you. And you know what, darling? If he doesn't, just forget him, you can do a lot better than him anyway. He's just a little drummer boy, after all.'

'What do you mean by that?'

'Oh come on, everyone in the industry knows that all drummers do is sit there and bash things! They just bang things for a living.' And so, in a vain attempt to try and cheer me up, Gavin sat there for the rest of the afternoon telling me 'drummer boy' jokes.

Ten days passed and I still hadn't heard anything. I was up in Leeds, where the band was due to play at the Heineken Free Festival along with Pulp, Sleeper and Menswear. Usually I loved the run-up to a major gig like this. There was always so much going on and I liked the camaraderie of these events. Invariably the acts would all be put up at the same hotel, and it was fun hanging out with the other bands. There would be late-night drinking sessions in the bar and impromptu parties in each other's rooms, and there were always drugs around. But I wasn't having a good time: I was miserable and morose, and I just wanted to be at home, away from it all. I was beginning to think I should just forget about Danny and write off our brief affair once and for all, but I couldn't. He may only have been 'a little drummer boy' as far as Gavin was concerned, but he meant the world to me and I wanted to be with him.

On Saturday afternoon, when we had finished our set and come off stage, a friend of mine called Danielle, who I was sharing the flat with at the time, rushed up to me.

'I've got a message for you!'

'Really,' I said unenthusiastically, assuming that it was probably from my mother. I wasn't in a good mood. My heart just hadn't been in the set. My voice had gone, and my performance had been mediocre at best.

'Danny called!'

'What?'

'He called the flat just before I left this morning. He said to tell you that he loves you, that he misses you loads and to call him when you can today.'

She handed me a scrap of paper. 'Here's his number.'

I stared at that scrap of paper, not knowing what to say. I couldn't believe he had called after all this time. I couldn't believe that he wanted to speak to me. That he *loved* and *missed* me.

We spoke later that night, just when I was going to bed and he was waking up. He told me that he had written a song for me called 'Late in the Day' and proceeded to sing it to me down the telephone. It was the most beautiful and romantic thing that anyone had ever done for me and I was deeply touched by the gesture. I had written him off, thought him to be heartless and uncaring, but he was nothing of the kind. We couldn't speak for long because he had to be somewhere, but he said that he was coming home in a week and that he wanted to see me as soon as he got back. We arranged that he would call when he landed and would come straight to the flat from the airport. I was relieved that things were fine between us, and I was so excited about seeing him again that I didn't know how I was going to make it through the week.

After what seemed like an eternity the day finally came. Danny was due to arrive at Heathrow that morning, and so I waited in the flat for his call. It never came. I waited all day but heard nothing. Maybe he was just delayed. Maybe he missed the flight. I ran through all the possibilities, but when he still hadn't called at midnight I gave up hope and went to bed. I couldn't sleep because I was just too upset and confused. I didn't know what was going on; I couldn't understand why he was treating me like this. Why keep making promises and plans if only to break them? Why blow so hot and cold? The following morning I thought about calling him in Oxford, but I decided that I wasn't going to chase him. He had made his point. I was upset and I was hurt, but I wasn't going to let him know that. I had to retain some modicum of dignity.

Two days later I was getting ready to leave the flat and meet up with Mark and Tim when the telephone rang.

It was Savidge and Best, our PR people. 'Are you with Danny Goffey?' they asked. If only I was.

'No, why? I asked.

'It's just we had a call from his manager trying to track him down. He said he thought he was with you. Is it OK if we give him your number? He seemed quite keen to speak to you, and maybe you could help?'

'That's fine, he can call me, but I'm telling you I haven't got a clue where he is.'

The telephone rang a couple of minutes later. It wasn't Supergrass's manager, it was Danny himself. He explained that when he arrived at Heathrow on Saturday he realised he had lost my number. Not knowing anyone who had it, he headed back home to Oxford. On Monday he set about trying to reach me via people in the industry and was eventually led to my publicity company. Too embarrassed to say he wanted my number for himself, he had pretended to be his manager. I couldn't quite believe what I was hearing, but I could tell from his tone that he wasn't making excuses.

'It's the truth,' he said. 'Why would I make a story like that up?'

I laughed.

'So, can I still come over?'

Danny arrived at the flat later that evening and we spent the next few days together. We hung out in London and then travelled to Glasgow, where we were both playing T in the Park. When we came back from Scotland we went on a weekend break to Brighton. We checked into a surreal hotel in the town centre where every room had a different theme. On our first night there we stayed in the Marine room, which had a waterbed, and on our second night we moved to the Brighton Rock room, which had a jacuzzi in the bathroom. We took strolls along the waterfront, ate seafood, went clubbing. We shopped for presents for each other and decided to have matching tattoos of a rainbow of stars done on our feet. We went to the pier and Danny won himself a fluffy dolphin in the arcade.

'I think I'll give this to Daisy,' he told me as we made our way back to the hotel. 'You are going to introduce me, aren't you?'

'You want to meet her?' I asked.

'Of course, why wouldn't I? She's part of you.' He stopped and kissed me.

Later that evening we took acid together and spent the rest of the night taking crazy photographs of ourselves. It was one of the best weekends of my life, and I can honestly say that I had never felt happier.

Over the following weeks our relationship grew stronger and stronger. Danny took me back home to Oxford and introduced me to his family and friends, and he in turn met Daisy when she returned from America. Danny had kept telling me how much he loved children, but I was still worried about how they would get along. It's easy to like kids when you only see them from time to time, quite another thing when they are around all day and night. I was nervous about how Daisy would adjust to the situation as well. Other than Owen, I hadn't had a serious relationship since my marriage broke down. For a time it had just been the two of us on our own, and I knew she liked it that way. Because of my schedule with the band Daisy spent most of the week with my parents, and so the time we had together was incredibly precious as it was. I didn't want her to feel threatened by the presence of someone else in my life, to feel that I was going to love her any less because I had found a boyfriend.

I needn't have been concerned. Daisy loved Danny right from the start, and he adored her. Daisy had found herself a new playmate in Danny, and he was such a big kid himself that he was happy to oblige. My friends took to him straight away. Although we didn't see much of Gavin during our first few months together as he had gone back to LA, he got on with the rest of my group. Zoë really liked him and he quickly bonded with Steve. My parents also approved. They liked the fact that he and Daisy got on so well and were relieved that I had at last found someone to love and who also loved me. My mother told me she had never seen me so happy.

Danny and I soon became inseparable. On the nights that my mother had Daisy, I'd spend time with Danny in Oxford at the house he shared with the rest of his band on the Cowley Road, and when he was in London he would always stay with me. We were lucky that because of our work we often performed at or attended the same gigs and festivals. In our first few months together, as well as appearing at T in the Park in Glasgow, we were amongst the bands playing at La Route du Rock in St Malo, in France, and we went to Reading together.

If there was one single thing I liked most about Danny back then it was his insatiable appetite for life. He was determined to live it to the full. All he wanted was for everyone around him to have a good time, and he was constantly thinking up little ruses to ensure that we did. He would dress up in silly clothes to make me laugh, he would pull pranks on his friends and would have us all in stitches with his endless jokes. He was always pulling funny faces and putting on accents. Everything was a game and an adventure to him. If we went out to dinner together on our own, to liven things up he would make us pretend to be other people, brother and sister, or two strangers who had just met for the first time. When we were in St Malo for the music festival he transformed what would otherwise have been quite a standard work trip into a holiday. Instead of hanging out with the other bands in bars and restaurants he insisted we went on a trip to the beach, and on the way there purchased buckets and spades, masks and snorkels and a beach ball. Life with Danny was a continuous rollercoaster of high-octane fun. Unlike so many people in the industry he didn't care about what people thought of him. He wasn't image or style conscious, he wasn't arrogant or full of attitude. He didn't brag, he didn't bitch about people and he wasn't into backstabbing. What you saw was what you got with Danny, and I loved him for that.

Within just a couple of months of our first meeting, Danny moved out of his house in Oxford and came to live with me in my flat in Primrose Hill. By some people's standards it may have appeared an impetuous decision, as we hadn't known each other for very long, but for us it seemed like the most natural move in the world. From the start of our relationship I knew that in Danny I had found my soul mate, and fortunately for me he felt the same way. We were in love and wanted to spend as much time as we could together.

9

Pretty Ugly

Our first few months together were one long, blissful honeymoon for Danny and me. Apart from when we had to honour our respective work commitments we never left each other's side. We spent our days off lying in bed together, our nights either painting the town red or setting the world to rights on our own, our time with Daisy going for walks or on outings. We cooked for one another, played games, wrote songs, went out for meals and to gigs. We shared a love of food, of film and, of course, a passion for music. And the fact that we both had the same career at first seemed to work in our favour as a couple, for we understood both the pleasure and the pressure of the world that we were in. And there was one other thing that Danny and I discovered we had in common during those first halcyon days together — and that was a taste for drugs.

Like me, Danny never had any social or moral issue with drug-taking. He didn't see that there was anything wrong in them, or why they should be outlawed in any way. If he wanted to get high, then that was his own personal choice and no one was going to tell him otherwise. He believed, as I did, that so long as you kept it under control then taking drugs with your friends was nothing more than a laugh, no different from enjoying a drink or two: it was just about having fun. Right from the beginning of our affair drugs had played a significant role in our relationship. Within hours of meeting each other at Dour we had taken ecstasy together. On our second date we had used cocaine. Throughout that first week together we had been almost perpetually stoned. When we went on our break to Brighton we tripped on acid.

Danny, like the true rock and roll boy he was, frequently seemed to have drugs on him, whether it was a gram of coke or speed he had scored from a friend, a couple of tabs of E or the end of a joint stashed away in his jacket pocket. If we were on a night out there always seemed to be something around, and if there wasn't then he would set about tracking some down. I didn't mind. I liked his sense of recklessness and I also liked my drugs. But whilst getting out of it was something of a common pursuit for Danny and me, our capacity for drugs was very different. It took very little for me to get high, but with Danny it was another story. He could take drug after drug and still seem to be in control. Whereas I, for example, could only cope with a line of coke before ending up completely wired, Danny could take four or five and still be making sense at the end of the night. He very rarely got hung over or suffered from bad come-downs. He would simply sleep off his night out the following morning, and by the afternoon would have bounced back to his normal happy-go-lucky self. I often wondered where he got his stamina from. Was he able to party harder than me because he was that much younger? Was it because he was heavier, or because he was a man? Or was it because he drank, and the alcohol he consumed somehow subdued the effects of the drugs we took? I never could quite work it out. Yet even though I was well aware that I was no match for Danny when it came to the amount of drugs we took, I still for some reason tried to keep up with him, line for line, pill for pill, joint for joint. I wasn't trying to impress him, I just wanted to hang out with him and have as much fun as possible.

Now that Danny had moved into my life I was using far more frequently than I had done before. I still considered myself to be a recreational user because I only took them when we 'partied', but the problem was there seemed to be a party just about every night of the week and the invitations just came flooding in. Whereas, in the past, I would have spent at least three or four nights each week taking it easy in the flat, going on trips to the movies with girlfriends or having dinner with my parents, I now had very little down time. The only evenings I stayed in were when I had Daisy for the night, otherwise Danny and I would be out and about, working the scene.

At first it was fun. Danny was a very sociable person and loved nothing more than meeting people and making new friends. He was so easy to like and get on with, our social circle seemed to expand on an almost daily basis. There was always something to do when he was around, some plan to be had, some great night out that we simply couldn't miss out on. I was happy to go along with it. As far as I was concerned we were having the time of our lives, and why not? I suppose, by most people's standards, our lives may have appeared to be a little dissolute, hedonistic even, but then we were not 'most' people. We were two young rock and roll kids living the myth. During those months I never once questioned the way we led our lives. Though we both had a reputation for being slightly wild and crazy, our behaviour at that stage was no more extreme than that of most of our friends.

I may have convinced myself that I was able to cope with the rock and roll lifestyle, but there was no question that my partying was starting to have an effect on me. Unlike Danny I found it difficult to bounce back from a night on the tiles. I could become quite introverted and morose when I was coming down, and be agitated and irritable the following day. I found myself becoming increasingly oversensitive about the most ridiculous things and was prone to bouts of paranoia, especially about the state of our relationship. If Danny spent the morning in bed after a heavy night out, for example, rather than simply conclude that he was tired and needed his sleep I would decide that he was ignoring me, or that he had fallen out of love with me. There were times when I would even shake him awake and insist on hearing reassurances from him before allowing him to go back to sleep. It was irrational, I know, but that's just how I felt.

And my partying, or to be more accurate drug-taking, wasn't just affecting my temperament, it was starting to have repercussions on my working life too. My attitude to the band changed almost overnight. In the past I had been fiercely ambitious for us. Powder was like my second child and I fought like a lioness for it. I was determined that we would succeed and that we would one day become a great name on the scene. I gave it my all and expected the others to follow my example. Now, because of the life I was leading, ambition gave way to apathy. I could no longer really be bothered with it all. I still liked making music and doing what we were doing, but I was no longer so interested in the other aspect of the band – the maintenance. I would turn up late to rehearsals because I was tired from the night before, and then leave early because there was something else I had to get to that evening. During our sessions I was tired and snappy. I found it difficult to concentrate on what we were doing, for my mind was forever elsewhere. All those late nights were starting to take their toll on my voice as well, the voice I had worked so hard to nurture and get right. My throat was often sore or croaky and I didn't have it in my lungs or myself to hit the right notes, to get the tone. Because I was tired I would sometimes skip press interviews, and on the occasions when I did manage to make them I was usually so hung over that I could barely follow the journalist's questions, let alone provide a witty, thoughtful or provocative response. In short I was quickly starting to have an amateurish approach to the profession I had once so desperately wanted, and I rather arrogantly and stupidly thought that I could get away with it.

In the days when I was starting out in the industry my one great dream had always been to play the Reading Festival. Some years before I formed Powder I had the privilege of seeing Nirvana perform there, and I remember being over-whelmed by excitement as they came on stage. The crowd broke out into an enormous roar as they took their places, and then, just before they started to play, it suddenly fell silent as if in a show of unanimous awe and respect for what we were all about to hear. And then, as they began to play their first song, the crowd went mad. It was one of the most electrifying and exhilarating things I had ever witnessed, and at that precise moment I knew that was going to be the one great goal of my career. I wasn't interested in playing Wembley, I didn't care about ever making it in America: all I wanted to do was to play Reading.

In the summer of 1995, just six weeks after meeting Danny, I finally got my chance. When we were told about the billing some months earlier and heard that we would be playing alongside Oasis, Blur, Elastica, Pulp, Echobelly and Menswear, it really felt as if we had arrived at last. The boys and I could talk about little else for days and immediately started to plan our set. We all knew this was it. The weekend of the festival finally arrived and Danny and I headed to Reading. It was Friday morning. Powder were due to perform the following day at 5 p.m. on the *NME* stage. It was a great slot for us, because it was late enough in the day for the crowds to have gathered but early enough in the evening for everyone not to be too mashed on drink and drugs. Danny and I arrived at the hotel, and as we were checking in we realised that we had been put up with all the other acts. In the bar we saw the likes of Oasis, Menswear and the Foo Fighters sitting there. In the lobby we bumped into some of our friends from Elastica, and coming out of the lift was a member of Blur. It was like a roll call of the best in British music, and I had to pinch myself to believe that I was actually there, included in it all. 'This is going to be such a scream!' I told Danny as we headed to our room. 'Can you imagine what the party is going to be like in here tonight?'

But Danny and I were far too impatient to wait and find out – we wanted the party to start right there and then – so once our room door had shut behind us the first thing we unpacked was our supply of drugs. We had brought a couple of tabs of ecstasy along with us, as well as a generous supply of cocaine and grass. It was always good to come prepared to a festival. We celebrated my début at the festival with a couple of small lines of cocaine, and later that afternoon popped an E. By the time evening fell we were both in flying form, and we went down to the hotel bar and partied hard with the other bands for a couple of hours.

It was tempting to carry on partying through the night, but I knew that I had to be at my best the following day, so at around two in the morning I decided to get some sleep. We went back to our room and smoked some marijuana in order to take the edge off the combination of coke and ecstasy we had taken, and eventually fell asleep. Before going to bed I had set my alarm for nine in the morning, as I knew that I had a lot to do that day before our set, but in the middle of the night I woke with a slight pain in my abdomen. I assumed it must be a cramp and that perhaps I was slightly premenstrual. I switched on the light so I could make my way to the bathroom, and as I did so I realised that I was bleeding. I assumed that I must have got my period in the middle of the night and once I had been to the loo I went back to bed. In the morning when the alarm woke me I felt a wet sheet underneath me. It was covered in blood.

Danny woke and saw the bedclothes. 'Oh my God! Are you OK?'

'I'm fine . . . I'm fine . . .'

'Should I get a doctor?' he said, looking at me rather helplessly.

'No, it's fine. It's just that time of the month, that's all.'

I went to the bathroom and had a shower. When I had

finished I wrapped myself in a bath towel and sat there for a moment whilst I got dry, but when I stood up to go back into the bedroom I realised that the bath towel was soaked in blood as well. It was slowly beginning to dawn on me what was going on. Just a couple of weeks before we went to Reading I had visited my doctor, because my coil had become misplaced and I needed to have it removed. During the consultation I had been warned that I should be careful in the following weeks because there was a slight possibility that I could be pregnant, and if that was the case then there was a chance I could miscarry. I told him I would be careful but thought very little about it afterwards. Now any woman in her right mind would have realised and called for a doctor at this stage, but because of all the drugs I had taken the night before I'd lost all sense of reason or judgement. Danny kept asking if I was all right through the bathroom door – I am not sure he had ever experienced anything like this in his life before – but I kept assuring him that I was OK.

I went back into the room and got dressed. I ate a little breakfast but was feeling very weak and was in quite a lot of pain. I asked Danny to roll me a joint, hoping that it might ease my stomach cramp. After an hour or two we made it out of the hotel. I took a bag with me with a couple of changes of clothes for my performance and we made it to the festival ground. I was feeling very drained and wasn't sure whether I had enough energy to get through the afternoon, let alone the performance, and so I decided that the best thing I could do at that stage, to give me the lift that I needed, was some coke. Danny and I found a secluded area at the back of one of the tents and we both took a line. But the line didn't give me the lift I needed, so I thought I'd take more. In the space of two hours I must have consumed nearly half a gram of cocaine, which was more than I had ever taken in my life. The drug was at last having an effect on me. As my pain numbed I felt much stronger, but the bleeding hadn't stopped – if anything it was getting heavier. I was reluctant to tell Danny what was going on, because I knew how protective he would be. He would probably insist that I pulled out of our set, and I wasn't going to miss this opportunity for anything in the world. It didn't matter what was happening to my body, the show had to go on. It was completely idiotic of me, I know, but at that point I was beyond thinking straight. I had so many drugs running through my system that I had lost all sense of reason.

At 4.45 p.m. the band and I were called backstage. I had already changed into my stage clothes and was trying my best to compose myself before the set. I took a deep breath and brushed myself down. Suddenly I realised that there was blood on my dress and, to my complete horror, it showed. I started searching for my bag in a panic. I had another dress on me, which fortunately was black. Although I knew I didn't have enough time to make it to a loo and then back to the wings before we were due to go on, I had no choice. I had to change.

By the time I got back to the *NME* stage I was half an hour late for our set. People backstage were screaming at me to get a move on.

'Where the hell have you been?' they shouted. 'You've totally screwed up the entire schedule!'

I'm not sure how I did it, but somehow I got through the set. When I came off stage I thought I was going to collapse, but I still refused to address what was happening to me.

'Are you sure you don't want to go back to the hotel?' Danny asked.

'No way!' I told him. 'What I would like now is to sit down and have a large joint and then I'll be fine.'

We walked off into the festival and found a place to sit by a lake on our own. We lit a small fire, took more drugs, cuddled up close together and listened to Neil Young play. It was then that I started to cry.

'What's up?' Danny asked. 'Don't be upset. I think you did brilliantly out there today!'

'It's not that,' I muttered.

'Well, what's there to cry about then?' he said, putting his arm round me.

'I think I've had a miscarriage.'

When we got back to London the next morning I went straight to hospital. Danny was beside me when the doctor confirmed that I had lost the baby. I went to bed later that day and he stayed with me, holding my hand as I sobbed into my pillow. I was upset because of the miscarriage, feeling low because I was coming down from the drugs, and sad because Danny was leaving for America the following day and would be away for six weeks with his band. It was all just too much.

The following day the reviews of the festival were published. My picture appeared in one of the papers, which I suppose was a plus, but in the accompanying article we had been slated. Playing Reading had always been my big dream, the thing I lived for; this was the gig that really mattered to me, but in one fell swoop I had ruined it, not just for myself but for the band as well. I was devastated.

A View From The Wings

Although Powder were not particularly well known outside of the indie music scene, within it we enjoyed a certain amount of notoriety, so I wasn't that surprised when Danny later confessed to me that he had known exactly who I was when he asked me my name in Dour that morning. What did take me slightly aback, however, was his admission that he had once cut my photograph out of a music magazine because he liked the look of me. I was flattered, and even slightly amused. In the early summer of 1995 Powder were the more established of our two bands and, as such, were better known, but that dynamic was soon to change, for within just weeks of our first encounter Supergrass's début album went to number one. Suddenly, this hitherto unknown group of boys from Oxford became one of the biggest bands on the scene.

Such was the buzz surrounding Supergrass in those first few weeks that it was difficult to turn on the radio without hearing one of their songs play; their videos seemed to be constantly on the music channels, and their faces stared out from the covers of magazines. Danny's phone never stopped ringing; there were requests for interviews, photo shoots, television appearances, gigs and quotes, and invitations to parties from people we had never met nor heard of. There is no denying that we were excited and thrilled by it all, but I am not sure whether either of us was really prepared for the impact that all this would have on our lives. I think we both assumed that once the album eventually slipped down the chart, interest in the band would also die down and we would go back to leading our lives as normal, but it didn't. With every passing week Supergrass just seemed to get more popular, and as their profile grew, so too did their schedules. They were constantly on the road now, playing gigs and festivals both here and abroad. They travelled all over Europe, went to the Far East, and played in America.

I was happy for Danny. He had achieved everything he had wanted, everything *I* had wanted for myself, and I was full of admiration for him. He deserved all this. He had worked hard for it since he was a teenager and the boys had first put the band together. How could I not be pleased for him? I loved him, so all I wanted was the best for him. But, exciting as this time was, I cannot pretend that there weren't moments when I wished that things could revert to how they had been before he hit the big time. For the fact is, however glamorous it might seem to date a young famous rock star, the actual reality of it is quite different. It can be quite a lonely and demoralising experience. It isn't much fun being away from your partner for a six-week stretch, unable to call when you want or need to because of their commitments or the time difference. Knowing that they are at a party surrounded by models and groupies and imagining the scenarios that might be taking place isn't exactly great for one's self-esteem when you are lying in bed alone at night. Stealing nights away together in sterile airport hotel rooms so you can be with your boyfriend before he flies off to yet another location isn't particularly romantic either. And when they aren't abroad, on the road or holed up in a recording studio, and you do get them home alone, then they are invariably asleep, because they are shattered. All in all, it is hardly the healthiest basis for a new relationship.

Danny and I made the most of the situation we found ourselves in. When he was away we kept in constant telephone contact, and when he went to America after the Reading Festival I joined him in San Francisco. We had a magical week together sightseeing, partying and catching up, but when our time together drew to a close I felt a sense of despair. I couldn't cope with the thought of going home without him, nor the realisation that it would be a whole month before we saw each other again. I tried to keep a lid on my emotions when Danny waved me off at the airport, but as soon as I reached the departure lounge I burst into floods of tears and continued to cry the whole way back to London. I threw myself into work as a means of distraction, but that didn't last very long, for as soon as Danny returned to London all I wanted to do was to be with him. As he didn't have that much free time to spend with me, I found myself trailing after him and the band. I went to interviews with them, followed them to gigs, even went on a trip to Germany. It went against my principles to follow a man round like this – I should have been getting on with my own thing, asserting a degree of independence – but I knew that if I wanted to be with Danny, this was the only way.

None of this was very easy for me. Before I met Danny I had been someone in my own right, I had an identity of my own. I had forged a career and earned a reputation. I'd been in the press, I'd been on the radio and television. When I performed at a gig fans might stop me and ask for my autograph. Of course, it hadn't reached the stage where I was being stopped on the street, but if I went to a club or a festival, let's say, then there would be people there who recognised me. 'That's Pearl from Powder,' they might say, or they might come up and tell me how much they liked our music. I had been flying high in my own little world, and I admit that I rather enjoyed living with my ego for a time. But as Danny's star continued to ascend, mine began to wane. Suddenly I was no longer a rock act, but relegated to the lowly and slightly degrading status of a rock chick. I went from being Pearl from Powder to being referred to as Mrs Supergrass, a moniker I loathed. I was now known primarily for being someone's girlfriend and I was not very comfortable about that.

My self-esteem took a huge battering. I remember when I accompanied Danny to Germany, sitting on the tour bus one afternoon thinking, what on earth am I doing? I hadn't seen Danny all day because he had been busy with press interviews, meetings and sound-checks. All I had done was wait for him – all I ever seemed to do these days was wait. I was bored and lonely, and I resented the fact that I felt like some crazed groupie, with nothing better to do than spend their life following the band. And then there was the time that I went with Danny to the BBC because the band were due to record a session of *Top of the Pops* and prepare for an appearance on some children's television show the following morning. I stood in the corner of the studio all day while people flocked around the band and pandered to their every need and whim, and no one even said so much as a hello to me. Even when Danny introduced me to them, no one asked me if I was OK, or whether I would like a cup of tea, or a chair. They knew I was there, but no one even acknowledged me. It was as though I was nothing, no one: I was invisible, like mist.

Perhaps it was slightly petulant of me to feel this way, but I wasn't ready to be cast to the sidelines or be condemned to a life of rock widowhood just yet. Naturally, I was glad that Danny was doing well. I was pleased for his success and wanted to be as supportive of his career as I possibly could, but as the months went on I couldn't help feeling that my sense of identity was beginning to be eclipsed by his stardom. I had to compete with so much on a daily basis to keep our relationship going that I was on edge. If I wasn't shuffling my life around his schedule, then I found myself having to compete with other people for his attention. I never begrudged the time he spent with his band; as a singer I knew how important that was. What I didn't really appreciate was the time he had to give over to others within the industry: the management, the press, the promotions people. It was as though I was forever at the back of the queue, waiting for an audience with *my* boyfriend. Our time together was becoming increasingly precious and so I resented it when I felt people took that away from us. Danny was a popular person, far more affable and easy to get on with than I was, and so there were always people around him. This was fine up to a point, but there were times when it got to me and I longed for the moments when I could have him to myself, back at our flat in Primrose Hill, cooking supper together, watching movies on TV, playing records. I remember feeling particularly frustrated in San Francisco one night when after dinner a whole group of people descended on our hotel room for an impromptu party. In normal circumstances I wouldn't have minded, because they were friends of ours, people from the music industry who like Danny were out there for the festival, but that night I did mind, because we only had one more day together before I went home. Luckily Danny was sensitive enough to pick up on this and suggested they went elsewhere, but when I went to bed that night I felt very blue.

It was getting to the stage where I seemed to constantly have to vie for his attention, and I was getting weary of it. We would go to a party together and as soon as we walked through the door we would find ourselves separated by a sea of people all wanting to get a piece of Danny. Because of what he did, men instantly wanted to befriend him; there was something of a laddish camaraderie when it came to drumming. Women would sidle up to him, completely impervious to the fact that he not only had a girlfriend but she was there, and I would find myself physically shunted out of the way by these little glamour pusses. And if all this wasn't enough to deal with, then there were the fans. They would camp outside the flat just to get a fleeting glimpse of him walking out of the front door. They would ring on the doorbell at all hours of the day or night, asking if he was there. On one occasion they wrote 'I love you Danny' in pink lipstick all over my Golf convertible. I was livid.

I tried to make the best of things and carried on with my life. I continued with the band. Danny was encouraging. Although he was enjoying the band's success he thankfully didn't give too much credence to his new-found status, and kept reminding me that all that really mattered was making music that you were proud of. He was right, but there was no question that the disparity between our careers was getting deeper day by day. I would be playing a tiny gig in some provincial town, staying in some grotty B&B, whilst he would be in London performing at some great venue, and put up in a swanky hotel. I remember one night when I was on tour in Birmingham cadging a lift back to London on another band's bus just so that I could get back to London and be with Danny. Supergrass were collecting a prize at the Q Awards at the Grosvenor House Hotel the following morning and I wanted to be there. When I arrived at the Park Lane Hotel, where Danny had been put up for the night, and walked into his room, I was stunned by just how different our lives had become in such a short period of time. When I performed away from home I was lucky even to be put up in a B&B, rather than have to travel back to London, but when he was booked in for a gig then it was five-star hotels all the way.

I hadn't been invited to the Q Awards, but that wasn't going to deter me from going. After dropping an E with Danny at nine in the morning I crashed the event. Much to his delight Danny had been put on a table with his idol Morrissey, and Cher was there too. High as a kite and with nowhere to sit, I spent much of the ceremony wandering round the room. Eventually I stumbled on Chris Evans, whom I had never met before, introduced myself and spent the rest of the show perched on his knee, telling him how much I loved him. He didn't seem to mind; if anything he appeared to be rather amused by my heightened state of excitement. Cher and Morrissey, however, shot me looks of total disdain when I finally made it back to Danny's table.

December came, and Supergrass had been booked to appear on Jools Holland's Hogmanay Special. It was always a great honour for any band to get a billing on Jools's programmes, let alone this particular one, so when the call came through both Danny and I were elated. Though it was to be broadcast on New Year's Eve, the show was prerecorded, but that did nothing to dampen the party atmosphere in the studio that night. Everyone was having the time of their lives, everyone except me. I did enjoy myself initially, meeting people, hanging out, listening to the music. When Supergrass went on to perform their set, I cheered like mad and felt immensely proud of Danny. When they finished I rushed up to congratulate him, flinging my arms around him and kissing him, but rather than return the act of affection, Danny just stood there impassive.

'What's up with you?' I asked, slightly bemused by his behaviour. 'Anyone would think the world had just ended.'

For a moment he said nothing and just stood there, looking at first distracted, then agitated. 'Look, I think we need to have a talk about something,' he ventured quietly. At once the phrase 'have to talk' hung in the air like a bad, almost suffocating stench. Despite the noise from the set I could hear nothing except those three words. My heart started to pound, my breath shortened. I knew that this was going to be bad.

'Let's sit down,' he said, pulling up a chair. 'I don't know how to say this, I've thought about it for a couple of weeks now . . . thought about not telling you at all, but I have to be honest with you because I can't be anything but with you . . . I've been unfaithful to you. I was unfaithful in America.'

For a brief moment the world seemed to stand still.

Everything stopped. And then suddenly it started up again. My head was spinning, I felt a lurch in my stomach, as though I was going to be sick.

'You what?' I whispered.

'I was unfaithful,' he repeated nervously, unable to look me in the eye. 'But you know, it meant nothing, absolutely nothing to me. I know that's a cliché but it's true. I love *you*, no one else, there is no one else.'

My eyes brimmed with tears. All my worst nightmares had been realised. I wanted to scream, but I couldn't. I wanted to shout at him, tell him how much I hated him, but I couldn't speak. Danny was upset. He looked confused, as though he might cry too.

'Look, I'm sorry. I really am. I didn't want to hurt you like this but I had to tell you. I didn't want to lie to you. I didn't want you to hear from someone else.'

I am not sure where the conversation went from there, what else was said. All I remember was grabbing my coat and bag and somehow making it home on my own. When I got back to the flat I packed up Danny's possessions and put them in a case, which I left in the central hallway. The rest of his stuff I threw out of the window.

I vowed that night never to have anything more to do with him. That was it, it was over. All the trust I had for Danny had gone, I simply couldn't love him any more. When he rang on my bell later that night, I screamed out the window for him to leave me alone and go away. When he called me on the phone I hung up. I wasn't standing for this. I wasn't having it. How dare he do this to me? How dare he betray me and ruin everything we had for some cheap fling with some little tart? It was over. I would never see him again. I would never let him back, I told myself and anyone who'd listen.

But rather than side with me, as I thought they would, my friends and family tried to make me see reason. Danny and I may have been together for six months when he told me, but when this happened we had only been dating for eight weeks. It was early days for us, they said. The fact was, he had been honest about it and that was what mattered. He could easily have covered his tracks and never told me, but he had been truthful and shown genuine remorse. People made mistakes, they said, and they told me in no uncertain terms that I would be a fool to let him go – I should give him a second chance. I took what they said to heart and considered what I had to lose. I didn't want the relationship to end, I didn't want Danny out of my life, I wanted to be with him always – and so when he sat on my doorstep for three days in a row pleading with me on the phone and via my intercom to take him back I gave in. I was still angry and hurt, but at the end of the day my love for him outweighed these emotions.

When I eventually let him into the flat Danny pledged his love for me and promised that it would never happen again, and I forgave him. Three weeks later we spent our first Christmas together. We took Daisy on a short trip to Lapland to see Father Christmas and then spent the holiday itself in the flat. We put up a tree, bought and wrapped presents for one another and cooked lunch. It was as though we were a proper little family and I loved every moment of it.

It was around this time that I decided that I no longer wanted to be in the band. Much as I had loved it to start with, I realised that my heart was no longer in it. I no longer cared for what we were doing, whether we were a success or not. I still wanted to make music but I simply couldn't cope with trying to juggle my career with Danny's. I wanted to be with him, and wanted to have Daisy back in my life – living with me – and for that to happen I knew that something had to give. For a time I struggled with the decision, but when I weighed it up I knew where my priorities lay.

I was apprehensive about telling Mark. From the start Powder had been as much his baby as it had been mine. I knew that he was going to be angry and regard it as unprofessional of me to put my feelings towards a boy before the band. I just didn't know how to break it to him, and so for a couple of weeks I put off telling him, but then in February I found my perfect way out: I was pregnant.

I assumed that Danny would be furious when I told him the news. He was so young and his career was just taking off; I thought the last thing he wanted was to become a father, but I couldn't have been more wrong. He was absolutely delighted by the prospect. We had put our problems behind us, and the prospect of having a child together heralded a new beginning and brought us closer together.

Mark, however, was less pleased.

'So, you're going to have a baby, then.'

'Yes, that's right.'

'So that's the end of the band?'

'I think so. I just can't see myself doing both.'

'OK. Well, I guess that's it then,' he said, before wishing me luck.

I didn't really care that my career with the band had come to an end. I was happy to turn my back on the industry for a while and relished the fact that I was about to become a mother again. I loved the idea of being barefoot and pregnant, of carrying Danny's child. Nothing else mattered to me at that time. I felt secure and loved and complete.

Alfie was born at the Portland Hospital on 9 October 1996. I was delighted to have a son, and Danny was over the moon. He was there for the birth but shortly afterwards was whisked off to the BBC. The band had another single out and he was due to appear on *Top of the Pops*. When he came back later that evening I was resting in bed in my private room.

'Guess what I was given tonight!' he said, kissing me.

'I've no idea, tell me,' I replied wearily.

He pulled out a wrap of coke from his trouser pocket.

'Where on earth did you get that from?'

'Some guy gave it to me at the show, a little present to say congratulations for having a baby.'

'I thought it was traditional to give the father of a newborn a cigar.'

'I know!' He put it back in his pocket.

'Can't I have a little line now?' I pleaded. It had been a straightforward labour but I was tired and thought that I could do with a pick-me-up.

'You are kidding, aren't you?'

'No. Someone told me the other day that it was fine to drink or take drugs before your breast milk came through. It's true. It's safe until then.'

Danny was unsure, but eventually I talked him round. I hadn't used anything whilst I was pregnant and had felt extremely good as a result, but this was all too tempting.

'OK, but just a tiny one,' he said.

Having taken a line in my bathroom, Danny and I then crept along the corridor to take a look at our baby son through the nursery window. Outside we bumped into the duty nurse. I was so excited by our new arrival and so high from the small amount of coke I had just consumed that I spent the next couple of hours sitting on a chair in the nurses' station telling the poor woman how much I loved my boyfriend, my daughter, my baby son and my life. But it wasn't just the coke talking – that is how I honestly felt.

We didn't have to announce Alfie's birth in the broadsheets, for the *NME* had already taken care of that for us. In what was an unprecedented move for them at the time they ran a small news story to mark his arrival, giving his name, weight and date of birth. 'Mother and baby doing well,' it read.

11

Going Nowhere

By the time Alfie was born Danny had started to reap the financial rewards of his success. We suddenly found ourselves in a position where we could afford our dream home, a beautiful white stucco four-bedroom house in Stratford Villas in the heart of Camden, and moved in when Alfie was three months old. Now that I was no longer working with the band I had time for my family and I wanted to create the perfect home for Danny, Alfie and Daisy, who, to my great joy, had moved in with us. I had fun buying pieces of furniture and objects for the house and selecting fabrics and finishes. We bought a brand new car and wardrobes of designer clothes for ourselves. I would visit Selfridges once or twice a month, and if I saw a dress or a pair of shoes that took my fancy, I would buy it there and then. I never thought twice about whether I needed it or could afford it. The children, though by no means spoilt, had everything they could possibly wish for. Compared with what Daisy had when she was a tiny baby, Alfie lived like a little king.

Danny and I ate out regularly. When we first met we might have called in a take-away or made a trip down to the chip shop, but now we were booking tables at some of the most exclusive and expensive restaurants in London. We went to the Ivy, the Caprice, out for sushi and dim sum, and we drank in private members' bars and clubs. I frequently went out to lunch with friends, more often than not picking up the bill, and I thought nothing of blowing £50 on breakfast at our up-market local café at weekends. It was all quite grown-up and a far cry from the life we led just a year earlier.

Danny and I had a wide circle of friends, one that included actors, models, artists, people from the world of fashion and photography, and we led a hectic social life. If we weren't out with our peers on the music scene then there were dinners with friends such as Sadie Frost, whom I had known since my teens, and her boyfriend Jude Law, and through him we got to know actors such as Ewan McGregor, Sean Pertwee and Jonny Lee Miller. We were close to Kate Moss, whom I met when she was dating the photographer Mario Sorrenti, and we hung out with Liam Gallagher and Patsy Kensit. Through Danny I met and formed a lifelong friendship with Liv Tyler. Glamorous as this coterie was, however, we always remained close to our roots. Zoë was still like a sister to me, and Danny spent time with his band and other old friends from Oxford.

Because of his status on the music scene we suddenly found ourselves fixtures on the celebrity circuit. We were invited to events and parties outside of the industry. We went to fashion launches, art openings, store events and film premières. There were invitations to restaurants and exclusive nights out at clubs. We were given discount cards to designer boutiques, free theatre tickets, courtesy cars and invariably, at the end of a night out, a large goody bag filled to the brim with luxury items: beauty products, clothes, handbags, cameras and even mobile phones.

Thanks to the success of Supergrass we were flown out to LA to visit Stephen Spielberg, who was interested in doing a television project with the boys. Not only were we invited to spend the day with him at his mansion, but we travelled first class and he generously picked up the bill. Naturally, at first all this was exciting for us. It's nice to be invited to fancy parties and delicious dinners in restaurants, and to have air stewards direct you left when you board a plane. Even though I didn't drink I liked the idea of being offered champagne everywhere we went or having a car wait for us outside a party. I enjoyed getting stuff for free – well, who wouldn't? And I would be lying if I said that there wasn't a certain thrill to be had when a press photographer took your picture at an event, or that it wasn't fun to have people catering for your every need. It was fantastic, and I have to say that at the time I was having a ball.

Although I had wanted out from Powder I knew that I didn't want to turn my back on music altogether. I decided I wanted to make a go of it again, and with Danny's help and encouragement we formed a new group with two members of a band called Delicatessen, Neil Cahill and Will Foster, and Danny came on board as well. We called ourselves Lodger. The boys from Powder didn't mind, for they had since moved on to other projects of their own.

Danny and I wrote a beautiful song called 'I'm Leaving' and within weeks of sending our first demo tape out we had five offers on the table. After some deliberation we signed a record deal with Island, which I was more than pleased about because I had always considered it to be my natural home. It was a generous deal, one that far exceeded my expectations as I had always thought of this as an artistic project rather than a commercial one. If that wasn't enough, Island paid for a full-time nanny to look after Daisy and Alfie, so I could get on with my music.

I should have been more than happy with my lot. I had very little to complain about, but after five months of this I started to feel quite dissatisfied about life in general. With the exception of Danny and my children I seemed to derive little pleasure from anyone or anything. I remember waking up one morning after we attended some extraordinarily glamorous party the night before and wondering whether I had actually enjoyed it or not. They had laid on vintage champagne and exquisite canapés. They had invited a whole host of A-list celebrities. Our friends had been there, and I had taken a little coke with one of them in the ladies' loo to get me into the party spirit. There had been a sit-down dinner, live music and dancing, and everyone seemed to be having a good time; everyone, that is, but me. As I lay in bed that morning I realised that I couldn't think of a single moment during the previous night when I truly enjoyed myself. In fact from the moment I checked my coat in I remembered feeling distinctly uncomfortable, and all I wanted to do was go home.

It was all supposed to be such tremendous fun, such a huge laugh, but the more we went out and the more we worked this scene, the more I started to question how much of a good time I was actually having. You would find yourself taking a seat at a film première and suddenly wondering what you were doing there. You didn't know anyone who had anything to do with the film, you probably wouldn't have chosen to see it if you were buying the tickets yourself, and yet you had dolled yourself up to the nines and travelled half-way across

London just to be there. You would tread the red carpet and have your picture taken, but for what? You knew it wouldn't be in the press the following day, because on the celebrity ladder you were still on the bottom rung. Wouldn't it be nicer to wait for the movie to be released and go to see it on a Sunday night in jeans and sweater? And wouldn't it be more entertaining to go out for a curry or a pizza with a group of friends afterwards rather than stand around looking aimless at an after-show party, surrounded by people you didn't know?

More often that not you would go to a party only to realise that it wasn't really a party at all – not in the way that most people would define one anyway. There was nothing to celebrate, no friend to toast, no talent to congratulate. It was nothing more than a product launch, a marketing exercise that you had been invited to attend simply because you were on a general list of people who went places, who accepted invitations like these. And on the way out, as you made your way to the coat check, you and your fellow guests would scramble for the goody bags, like vultures on their prey. But when you got home and unpacked the bag you realised in a slightly blasé fashion that there was nothing in it that you really wanted or needed. So there was a designer handbag, which must have been worth eight hundred pounds at least, but it was not the handbag you would have chosen had you gone out and shopped for it yourself, and there were beauty products too, but your bathroom shelves already groaned with the stuff. And so you would pack the bag up again and leave it in the hallway until you found someone who would appreciate it all. You see these parties in magazines and you think to yourself, 'How fabulous – Michael Caine was there!' but what you don't realise is that

Michael Caine was there for all of two minutes, and that even if you do go to a party he is invited to, you don't actually get to meet him. He will be ushered through the door, he will pose for the photographers, and then do a small circuit of the room before wisely leaving, as planned, to go and have dinner with his family and friends.

Even when we went to LA I found it hard to have a good time. Of course, it was amazing flying first class and getting to meet Spielberg himself, but once that introduction had been made and he started talking business with the boys, I suddenly felt very insecure about my presence there. I was conscious of the fact that I was nothing more than a hanger-on. Later that night we met up with Jonny Lee Miller. He was married to Angelina Jolie at the time and for all her warmth and friendliness, as we all sat down for dinner, I found it difficult to relax. She was so beautiful, so confident and so talented that it was hard not to feel slightly less than wonderful in her company, not least because I was seven months pregnant with Alfie at the time. She walked into the room looking both sylph-like and gamine with her cropped hair, while I sat there with my huge tummy feeling frumpy and matronly in my maternity clothes.

I wasn't really sure why I felt quite so despondent about everything at the time, it was quite uncharacteristic of me. I had always been so full of life and vitality before, always up for a good time and a party, but now I was finding it hard to raise even the faintest smile over anything. Maybe it was because I had lost my sense of expectation. After so many years of struggling I now had it all on a plate. I didn't want for anything or wish for anything. I had material wealth, I had my circle of friends and I had been given a second chance with my career without even having to try. But none of that really mattered to me deep down any more. What I cared most about was Danny and the kids, and the more we went out, the more we partied, the more I realised I just wanted to be with them. I hated kissing my children goodbye at night, I resented leaving them with the nanny; it just wasn't my style. I didn't want to be one of those mothers who air-kisses her kids at night for fear of smudging her make-up, who's never there for the bedtime story, always out the door. But because of the world that we were in, I felt I had to go out. And so I'd get dressed, put on my best fake smile and go out to the party, but once I got there I could never really have a good time for I was racked with guilt.

Shortly after we moved into our new house in Stratford Villas, Danny left to go on tour again. I had assumed, now that our relationship was steady and established, and I had the big family home and my children around me, that it would be easier this time round, but if anything it was worse. Danny called every day, but these conversations were often held at the mercy of time differences. If Danny was in America, for example, and called when he got up in the morning, I would usually be busy with Alfie and so didn't have time to stop and chat. If he called late at night, then I would be taking Daisy to school. There was nothing I liked more than being at home with the children, but I found that when we spoke on the phone and Danny asked me how my day had been, I wouldn't really have that much to say. He, on the other hand, was full of tales of the night before, of the gig, the festival, the music junket he had been to. If I told him about some domestic problem I was having he couldn't deal with it, which was fair enough. 'What can I do from here?' he'd say. 'I'll sort it out when I get home, I promise.' At times our conversations could be quite strained, and when it got like that I found myself creating arguments with Danny just to keep him on the phone. When he was away I spent a lot of time in tears. I was feeling lonelier than I had ever done in my life.

It was around this time that I started using drugs again. Now that I was no longer breast-feeding Alfie I felt I could indulge. At first my intake was quite controlled. I'd have a couple of joints in the evening to help me relax if I was staying in, or take the odd line of cocaine if I was out at night, but within just a matter of weeks my use started to get out of control. I was no longer relying on other people to give me drugs, I had started buying my own, something that I had never really done before with the exception of cannabis. And to make matters worse I had started smoking smack.

Since my first experience with heroin back at the beginning of my career I had experimented with the drug on a couple of occasions. Both times Danny had been with me and he had smoked it as well, but we had only had a couple of draws, for Danny was acutely aware of how addictive it was. He would remind me of this time and time again.

'Once in a while it's OK, but it's just not something one wants to get into,' he would say. 'It's not like other drugs. It's a slippery slope. You think you have it under control and then suddenly you're hooked. All it can take is a couple of smokes.'

And of course, Danny was right, because after just a couple of sessions smoking it I *was* hooked.

It all began when I befriended a girl who lived near us in Camden. She would come round when Danny was away, and once I had got the children to bed we would spend the evening together smoking joints. She was younger than I was and we didn't have that much in common, but I was grateful for the company. One night early on in his tour she said she had some heroin on her and asked me if I would like some. I thought about it for a minute or two, but then thought 'why not' – the children were in bed, the nanny was coming in the morning and I wasn't going anywhere. Just a couple of smokes would see me right, maybe lift my mood and help me sleep better. After a couple of hits my mood had improved, in fact for a few hours I had never felt happier. It was as though I had just been given a large shot of an antidepressant. Suddenly all my problems and worries disappeared. I didn't mind that Danny was away, I was happy for him. I didn't feel lonely or down, I felt blissfully content. I didn't sleep that night, but that didn't matter for I was enjoying the moment. Why sleep when you could feel like this?

After that night my friend started to visit me more regularly at my request. She brought her friends and her gear with her, and we would lie on my bed getting progressively out of it. It was heaven, and I looked forward to the evenings she came with great anticipation. But as the weeks passed and my appetite for the drug grew, these sessions became more frequent. I was smoking heroin two or three times a week now, and I soon realised that I didn't want to have to wait until she came round to use. I wanted to take it when I felt like it – morning, noon and night, if that's what I felt like – and so I took the number of her dealer and started buying my own gear and smoking it alone.

12

Crossing The Line

At first no one knew my secret. I couldn't share it with anyone, for I was aware that if they found out I would have to stop, and I certainly didn't want that to happen. Away touring, Danny was completely oblivious to what I was up to, and I made sure it stayed that way for if he discovered the truth I knew that he would freak out. I kept it hidden from Zoë because she would have vehemently disapproved, and away from our other friends because, however rock and roll they were, taking smack was taboo within our circle. The only people who knew about my predilection for heroin were the dealers who supplied me with the drug and the people I used with. We were a disparate gang, with nothing in common other than our shared love of opiates, but that didn't matter because once we were smoking we entered our own worlds. I had always been quite selective about my friends, but when it came to heroin I didn't have any such standards. All that mattered was that they used. They could be convicted criminals for all I cared – and indeed some of them were.

I had enjoyed those evening sessions with my drug buddies lying on my bed in a fog of intoxicating fumes, but because it is difficult to sleep on heroin I soon learnt that it was better for me to take it during the day than at night; that way I could function more 'normally'. Once Daisy had gone to school and the nanny was out with Alfie, I would call my dealer and have him come round. I would roll the drug up in cigarettes and smoke them round the house. Mindful of the fact that its fumes smelt like urine, and not wanting to get caught out, I would light scented candles and open all the windows before I started puffing away. If the nanny came whilst I was out of it, I would simply excuse my state of delirium by insisting that I was tired and would go upstairs for a 'little lie down'.

Even though I was using the drug quite regularly and taking it on my own, I still didn't acknowledge that I had a problem with it. I knew that I had developed a taste for heroin, but I didn't have a 'habit'. It was just something I did to make me feel better and happier about life, to relieve the boredom and fill my time while Danny was away. I knew that I wasn't addicted to the drug, because I only did it when the mood suited me and I could go for days if not weeks, when Danny was at home for example, without it. And I didn't take it when I went out at night. Not only would I have been too out of it to interact socially, but it would have been obvious to anyone I came into contact with what I was on. When you take heroin your pupils contract to the size of pin-heads, which is why people say you are 'pinned' on smack.

I categorically refused to see that I was dependent on heroin, or any other drug for that matter. All I was doing was dabbling. I didn't have a problem, I would tell myself, as I called the dealer back to the house for a second time in a day, as I chopped myself a line of coke or found myself gasping for a joint first thing in the morning. I was fine, just fine. Of course, I couldn't see what was happening to me, few people do. Addiction has a nasty way of creeping up on you like that and taking you by surprise. One minute you are the master, the next you are the slave, and while the switch from substance use to substance abuse can happen in an instant, it may take you a while to realise it. I didn't see I had a problem for a long time, and when I did read the signs I chose to ignore them.

The moment the penny dropped for me was when I was at a private party in the country after Danny returned from his tour. I was sitting at a table with a group of friends when one of them offered me a line of cocaine. I politely refused, not because I didn't want one but because I had my own supply and it looked like they were running out. People were openly using drugs at the party, so I had no qualms about emptying half of the contents of my wrap on to an empty plate and cutting it. I racked out five lines with the intention of sharing it out, and took the first. I was feeling slightly flat that night and I thought that I could do with a kick-start. Within minutes of taking the second I was on to the third, then the fourth. No one noticed what I was doing, they were far too gone themselves, too deep in their coke talk. As I bent over the table to snort my final line I remember clearly thinking, 'God, I'm an addict.' But that didn't stop me from cleaning the plate.

I bumped into Danny half an hour later. My heart was pounding, my face was gurning and I was talking gibberish. He took one look at me and knew.

'Just how much coke have you taken?'

All I could manage was a shrug.

Cocaine was a drug that just didn't suit me. Just as there

are good drunks and bad ones, I was a bad coke-taker. In general people use cocaine to make themselves feel more alert, confident and extrovert, but it had always had quite the opposite effect on me. I could get away with, and feel the benefits of, one line of the drug, but if I took any more I would become introverted, insecure and paranoid. Needless to say, that still didn't put me off it. Alcohol is known to subdue some of the effects of cocaine, taking the edge off it, but because I didn't drink I didn't have that balance. The effects of the drug on me were always extreme. It would charge me up, but I never had anything bar the odd spliff or two to bring me down. And yet even though I knew cocaine wasn't right for me, undeterred, I would take as much as the next person.

'You know you're not good on it,' Danny would say after my use of the drug had ruined yet another night out for us. 'You don't need to take as much as you do. When you're not on it you are this vibrant, happy person, and then as soon as you start overdoing it you just shut down.'

He was right, of course, but I chose not to listen, I just carried on. My dependency on coke was becoming extreme. I wouldn't go out to a party unless I knew I could get some, and because of that I always made sure that I had my own supply; I couldn't cope with the idea of running out. I would take it before I left the house in the evening to give me a boost, and I had started using during the day as well. I was no longer a recreational drug user. I had crossed that line some time ago. I now had a serious habit and was quickly hurtling towards full-on drug dependency.

Danny knew that I was overdoing it with the drugs, and he frequently told me to get my use 'under control', as he put it, but I don't believe he ever wanted me to get and stay clean. If I'd stopped taking drugs altogether, he would have had no one to play with. He was just as much in denial about the severity of my drug addiction as I was. And, in any case, he had his own moments when he went too far. There had been the family Christmas lunch where Danny had taken so much cocaine the night before that he got lockjaw. It was so severe that he couldn't bite, so we had to put his Christmas lunch, trimmings and all, in a blender.

'What on earth is wrong with him?' my sister-in-law asked.

'I haven't got a clue,' I said.

Not long after the party in the country Danny and I went to Oxford for another shindig. Once again I had taken coke with me and once again I had overdone it, and as a result I was feeling really crummy. My face was contorting, my heart was racing and I wasn't making much sense. A girl I knew on the music scene could see I was out of sorts, so she offered me a smoke to calm me down. At first I thought she meant grass, but when she whispered in my ear that she had smack on her I was delighted. We snuck upstairs, found an empty room and took a couple of hits. Within minutes I was feeling better, in fact I felt fantastic. My heart slowed down, my pulse stopped racing and when I rejoined the party twenty minutes later, even though I was high on heroin and cocaine, it was as though I was back to normal. I could talk to people, I could dance and I could enjoy myself. The heroin had taken the edge off the cocaine, and the cocaine in turn had given me energy that I wouldn't have had if I had just taken smack. At last, on this heady cocktail, I had found my balance.

Like anyone who has addiction issues I covered it up well.

I was the master of deception and conniving. In my relationship with Danny honesty had always been of the utmost importance, and yet now I was lying to him. I was always covering my tracks so that he wouldn't find out. Danny knew that I was buying drugs but he had no idea of the amount. He just assumed, when I pulled out a wrap of coke at a party, that it was all I had on me. When I polished it off later that night I would tell him that I had shared it with friends or that I had mislaid it. He didn't know about the other grams I kept stashed away in my drawer, the sneaky little line I might take when he was out for the day, the amount I went through when he was away, or the money I was spending each week on my habit – and he didn't know about the smack. But there was only so long that I could keep him in the dark. It was easy to live a double life while he was away, but when he was at home it got complicated.

The first time I suggested that we smoked heroin together he seemed quite up for it. He thought it might be a fun 'experience', like tripping on acid or taking mushrooms. And it was, for we had an amazing night together. I left it a while before I suggested that we did it again, but he was receptive to the idea. Had he known the extent of my habit at that stage, the fact that I was consuming £80 worth of heroin a day, which is a lot, then I know that he wouldn't have got involved, but as far as he was concerned we were just using it occasionally. For him, taking heroin was a luxury we indulged in every now and then.

Because I had a full-time nanny I was able to get away with my drug use. Without even having to be asked she took care of most aspects of life on the home front, so I had few responsibilities. The whole point of having childcare was to give me the freedom and time to work on the band, but I just used it as an opportunity to party even harder. Having help meant that if I had a heavy night taking heroin or coke, or a combination of the two, I could spend the rest of the day in bed.

I was so out of it that I didn't take my commitment to the band seriously, which was a waste because the first few tracks Lodger had released had met with critical acclaim. Island had invested hundreds of thousands of pounds in the band, but that meant nothing to me. If we had a studio session booked for the day, I wouldn't show up until the afternoon if I went at all. If I had an interview I'd be late. I turned up to photo shoots looking exhausted because I hadn't slept all night or like a monster because I was pinned. And I was incapable of making a sound decision about anything. I would ring Neil or Will late at night when I was as high as a kite and tell them my ideas for the band. When they called the next day to follow up on my decisions, or to have their say, I wouldn't have the faintest idea what they were talking about. I wouldn't admit it, blaming everyone else around me, but it was ultimately my fault that the band weren't going anywhere. There had been a flurry of excitement surrounding our single 'I'm Leaving', and as a result our first album was greatly anticipated by Island and the music press, but rather than seize the moment we stalled. By the time we did get it together to release eighteen months later we found that our sound was no longer so unique. There were a couple of other bands out there now doing the same kind of thing, and unfortunately it looked as though we had just jumped on the bandwagon.

As it was taking so long to record the album, I decided that the best thing we could do was go away to work on it. Danny, Will, Neil and I would take a month out and stay in the country and get it done. I had found a recording studio not far out of London that I liked the look of. I hadn't chosen it for its facilities; in fact I hadn't even visited it, as I should have done. I had selected it purely because on the cover of its brochure there was a picture of a man sitting in the sun by a swimming pool with a cocktail in his hand – that's how irrational I had become. That's the one, I thought, we'll go there. It looks like Miami.

Never had the adage 'don't judge a book by its cover' been so true. The afternoon we arrived at the studio it was pouring with rain. There was a pool, but we wouldn't be swimming in it even if the weather did improve, for it appeared that it hadn't been cleaned. The water was dark green and it smelt. The 'studio' itself looked like someone's living-room. The vocal booth was in a barn.

'What the hell are we doing here?' Danny screamed. 'There isn't even a proper drum room!'

I guess the others should have realised that my heart wasn't really in the project when they saw that I had brought my dealer along for the ride. Neil and Will were furious. 'But he's a really nice guy!' I said when they asked me what he was doing there. I spent most of my time up in my room taking drugs whilst they tried to make the most of the situation and the facilities. When I did come down to the studio and deign to take part in the sessions I would bite their heads off if they so much as offered me the slightest constructive criticism. It was all so chaotic that Danny and I resigned ourselves to the fact that we weren't going to get anything done and spent most of the time in the studio taking coke. Every morning we would take a large mirror off the studio wall, pour our coke on to it and rack out lines. We didn't think about hanging it up again when we left in the evening, we didn't even have the courtesy to wipe the coke off it. But every night the woman who owned the studio, and who was fast beginning to loathe us, would polish it clean and put it back on the wall again. She was livid with us, but not as angry as we were with her for wiping our coke away. We left soon afterwards. We had spent thousands and thousands of pounds and had nothing to show for it.

As my addiction worsened my behaviour became increasingly erratic. I would alternate between being happy one moment and depressed the next. I became aggressive and took my moods out on Danny. I no longer respected time differences or work commitments when Danny was on tour and would ring him at all times of the day and night, often screaming at him for no reason. Just as my drug use was ruining things for Lodger, it now started to cause problems for Danny with Supergrass. From the start of our relationship his management had been wary of me. They always suspected me of being something of a loose cannon, and now I was proving them right. I was becoming their very own Yoko Ono. I would make Danny late for meetings and rehearsals by insisting that he be with me. I would turn up to his sessions uninvited because I didn't want to be on my own. I was becoming a thorn in their side, but I simply didn't care. Every time he left to go on tour I would beg him not to go. 'Please don't leave me,' was a refrain that echoed throughout this period.

One morning in 1997 Danny was getting ready to leave the house to fly to Scotland. It was the start of his UK tour, and he had been looking forward to it as he was going to be playing alongside the American band Spacehog, who were friends of his. I had tried to make him stay behind again, but he refused point blank. Realising that he was not to be turned I offered to drive him to the airport, which was madness really as I had been up most of the night, had got very little sleep and was still feeling the effects of the drugs I had taken. Tired and hung over, I decided that I wanted to continue our argument in the car and was shouting at him at the top of my voice. After half an hour of this Danny lost his temper. 'That's enough!' he yelled, slamming his fist against the dashboard. He hit his hand down with such force that he cried out in pain. For once I was silenced.

By the time Danny boarded the plane his hand had swollen to the size of a melon. The little old lady who was sitting next to him on the flight was so concerned that she called the air stewardess for help. Danny spent the trip from London to Edinburgh with his hand submerged into a sick-bag filled with ice. When he landed he was in so much pain that he went straight to the hospital. He had broken his hand. With Danny unable to play, the band were forced to cancel the tour. They were devastated, not least because it was going to cost them hundreds of thousands of pounds. I, on the other hand, in my perverse way, was delighted. My wish had come true: Danny was coming home.

Despite my behaviour Danny still wasn't aware of the full extent of my drug use. If I was being aggressive he just assumed that it was because I was tired or unhappy. He put my mood swings down to the fact that I was going through a difficult time with work or the children. If I was withdrawing from heroin and started to shake or sweat, or feel and be sick, I would tell him that I had flu. 'Again?' he would say. 'That's the second time this month. I think you should see the doctor.' I always had an excuse at hand.

It wasn't until the summer of 1998 that I finally got rumbled. Danny was away again and I was lying in bed unable to sleep one morning when the doorbell rang. It was six in the morning. I got up and went downstairs to open it. On the step were two friends of mine who were hugely successful in the music industry. I had taken smack with one of them before, and she was as high as a kite when I let them into the house.

'Sorry to have got you up, Pearl. I wouldn't have done this if I wasn't desperate, but we were round the corner and I've run out of gear and was wondering if you could sort me out!' Although I was annoyed to be called upon at this hour in the morning, and loath to part with my supply of heroin, I knew how she felt. I had been there and it wasn't a nice experience, which is why I now kept a reserve supply. I went to my room, found my drugs and gave some to her and then sent them on their way.

Some weeks later Danny was performing at a festival when the man came up to him. 'I saw your missus the other day.'

'Really?' Danny said.

'Yes, she's a top woman. Sorted us out at six in the morning.'

'Sorted you out? What do you mean?'

'Yeah, you know, with some gear . . . some smack, really good of her to do that. X was withdrawing and she needed a pick-me-up.'

Danny didn't say anything. He didn't mention it when we spoke on the phone that night, but I could tell that there was something wrong. When he got back to London he had it out with me. He was enraged.

'What do you mean you had heroin on you?'

'I just had some lying around, some old stuff that we didn't finish,' I lied.

'You really expect me to believe that?'

'It's the truth!'

'Then try and explain to me how these people knew that you had it? Tell me how they knew? Have you got that much of a reputation that when people want to score they come to you like you are some kind of dealer?'

After this confrontation I decided to ease off the drugs for a while. This was not because I felt in any way contrite or guilty about my use, or because I wanted to, but because I wanted to get Danny off my back. It wasn't easy, though, and within weeks I had returned to my old habits again. One night when Danny was on the road again, my little friend, the one who had introduced me to heroin, came over and we sat up till the early hours smoking. At five in the morning we called it a night and she left to go home. I had seen her out of the door and was making my way up the stairs when I heard a crash and a scream. I grabbed my keys and hurried out of the house to see what had happened. She was lying there in a pool of blood in the middle of the road in front of a black cab. The cabbie was by her side, trying to see if she was conscious.

'It wasn't my fault,' he kept saying. 'I didn't see her. She just stepped out into the road, from nowhere, straight into the cab.'

We called an ambulance and got her to hospital. I thought she was going to die, but she pulled through. When she came round she was delirious and was asking for toot. 'What does she mean by toot?' her mother asked me. I said nothing. I left the room, found a doctor and told him. I explained that we had been up all night and that we had taken heroin. I was embarrassed but I knew that I had to be honest. 'You do realise that she nearly lost her life?' the doctor said. 'And that had she not been on drugs she wouldn't be in here?' I knew, of course I knew. It was all down to me that she was here. It was all down to the drugs. Looking back, that should have been the moment when I realised just how dangerous drugs were. I should have got clean there and then, but I didn't.

13

Save Me

To Danny's dismay I carried on using throughout the summer of 1998. He could see that I was unwell and thought that I should try to 'lay off' them for a while. Even though I chose to ignore him I knew he was right. I was beginning to reach the stage where even I had had enough. It wasn't the drugs themselves that I had tired of, but the life I was having to lead in order to take them. The late-night sessions, the sleepless nights, the constant hangovers were taking their toll on me. I was a physical wreck, a shadow of my former self.

I'd always been a great foodie. I loved to cook and I loved to eat. Amongst our circle I was famous for my roasts, so much so that it became something of a longstanding joke, for I never seemed to cook anything else. I loved the whole ritual of putting the meal together, taking two hours out of the day to make something special. I found it both relaxing and rewarding. But now that I was so heavily addicted to drugs I had given up that pastime. On heroin you couldn't eat, for it made you physically ill. Just one mouthful of food would make you vomit, so I avoided eating altogether when I was using and just drank water. If I had been on a heroin binge then I wouldn't eat for days. As a result my weight plummeted and I went from a healthy size ten down to a six within just a couple of months. Although I had never been fat, I had always struggled with my weight, so I was quite pleased with my svelte new figure. Danny wasn't so happy. He didn't think I looked svelte at all, he thought I looked like a skeleton and was concerned about my health.

Because I wasn't eating I was no longer getting the nutrients my body needed. My nails and hair became brittle, my skin was oily and I became prone to acne. I had never had spots in my life, but now I had a rash of them all over my forehead. It got so bad that I cut a fringe to cover it up. I had dark circles under my eyes from so many white nights. I could never get to sleep when I was using, it was impossible. Instead I would resort to downers and sleeping pills. Mogadons, Rohypnol, Valium, Xanax – I had repeat prescriptions for them all, courtesy of a doctor acquaintance who was happy to oblige. But it was never enough to take one sleeping pill to get me off, I had to take four or five. Danny used to joke that it would take a horse tranquilliser to get me off to sleep. I took so many pills at night that I sometimes wondered whether I would wake up in the morning. My teeth were stained from all the heroin I took, and I suffered frequent nosebleeds as a result of all the cocaine I snorted. Although my nose never collapsed, the lining of my septum was damaged and I had screwed my sinuses. My nose was always streaming, as though I had a permanent cold.

Mentally I wasn't much better. All the drugs I had taken had distorted any sense of perspective I once had. I got upset and paranoid over the slightest things. If someone didn't return my call promptly enough, for example, I decided that it was because they hated me. If Danny wasn't constantly telling me he loved me I concluded that it must be because he had met someone else. The more I let things around me go, the worse they became. I dodged calls that were to do with work, left faxes and letters unanswered. If a bill arrived, even though I had plenty of money in my bank account I wouldn't pay it, I wouldn't even open it. Instead I 'filed' the envelope in a drawer, alongside my unpaid parking fines, credit card bills and taxi receipts. I found lying to Danny exhausting. For all my skill in deception, I was growing weary of always having to come up with an excuse to explain away my behaviour.

'Why don't you just stop?' Zoë gently asked one morning when she popped over. Despite the fact that it was lunchtime I still wasn't dressed and was sitting in a heap on the sofa nursing yet another hangover. She had caught wind of my habit earlier in the year and had tried to confront me, but to no end. I had simply bitten her head off and told her that if she bleated on me to Danny our friendship was finished. Since then she had trodden carefully with me. She was concerned that if she tried to intervene then I would stick to my word, and she worried about what might happen then.

'I do stop from time to time. I went three months without it in the spring,' I snapped.

'I mean . . . stop for good. It doesn't seem to make you very happy.'

I knew that Zoë was right. Heroin wasn't making me happy and I should get clean, but the problem was that I didn't really have a strong enough incentive to stop. I'd enjoy the weeks when I was off drugs. I'd feel good about my life, the kids, Danny, work even, but good as these times were I always found myself going back to drugs. I believed I wasn't strong enough to say 'no', to give up once and for all. But that changed in September, when I discovered that I was pregnant again. Given what I had put my body through, it was a miracle that I ever conceived Frankie at all, but there I was, having another baby.

Danny was really happy about the news. He couldn't wait to have another child and believed that this baby might be the answer to his prayers. Maybe now I would calm down, find some inner peace and settle into family life. Maybe now our relationship, which had been severely compromised by my addiction, could get back on an even keel.

I too was delighted that I was pregnant. I may not have been the most conventional or responsible of parents, I may have been a drug addict, but that didn't mean that I didn't love my children. But there was another reason why I was so thrilled to be pregnant, and that was because I now had the incentive I needed to stay clean. No more smack, no more coke – I didn't even smoke a joint. Although my dependency on drugs was down to me, there was a lot of pressure to indulge in them because there was a general belief in our world that you couldn't have fun unless you were slightly out of it. But now I had the perfect excuse not to play the game. I enjoyed being in the position, when someone offered me a line of coke, of being able to turn them down. 'Not for me!' I would say in a superior tone. 'I'm pregnant, you know!' I knew people who had used drugs during their pregnancies, but that wasn't for me. There was no way I was going to compromise the health of my unborn child. I was full of the best intentions.

Then, when I was six months pregnant, Danny and I were invited to a huge society party in Paris, which was being thrown by someone high up in fashion. When I look back on it now I can see that it was the kind of event where you leave your soul at the door, but when the invitation came I knew I had to be there, for this was going to be the party of all parties. I had been to glamorous events in the past, but nothing came close to this. If there had been a theme for the night then it would have been sheer opulence.

Everywhere you turned there was a famous face: Hollywood stars, supermodels, famous photographers, film directors. Everyone in the room was beautiful; even the staff looked as though they had just sashayed off the catwalk. The food was to die for, the wine was exquisite, the atmosphere electric. After pudding was served the coke came out. Silver trays covered in neatly drawn lines of white powder were brought to the tables. Though not everyone partook, no one batted an eyelid. It was as if it was the most normal thing in the world to be served cocaine at the end of dinner, but then again, in the world that we were in, it was.

At first I refused. Stating what was blindingly obvious, I told the guest on my right who offered me the tray that I was pregnant and therefore couldn't indulge. But after an hour, temptation started to get the better of me and I began eyeing up the tray.

'It's OK to take cocaine when you are as far gone as you are,' a model told me.

'Yes, she's right,' chirped another female guest. 'I used during my pregnancy and my kid is fine. It's all a myth that you can't do anything when you're pregnant. So long as you don't do drink and drugs in the first trimester, then it's OK to do anything so long as it's in moderation.'

It wasn't just my soul that I left at the door that night, I must have left my mind there as well, because I decided to believe them. I was discreet about the first couple of lines I took, but by the third I was so blown away that I started using openly on the table. People looked on in horror. There I was, six months pregnant, wolfing the drug up like a coke whore.

'Good for you!' said the female guest. 'Enjoy yourself.'

Danny had been sitting at another table when this was going on. By the time he caught up with me I was about to take my fifth line. 'What are you doing?' he said with a look of horror when he saw me hovering over the tray with a straw.

'Lighten up, will you?' I said.

'Don't do it, please don't do it.'

But I didn't listen. When I was high I never listened to anyone, other than the little demon voice inside my head telling me to take more.

Danny grabbed me by the arm.

'What are you doing?' I protested.

'Taking you back to the hotel!' Much as Danny wanted to stay at the party he knew that the only way he could get me to stop was to take me out of the situation. When I woke the next morning at six I was so disgusted with myself that I tried to make myself sick. I couldn't believe that I had been so stupid, weak-willed and selfish. I felt so ashamed and revolted by what I had done that I wanted to get the hell out of Paris. I woke Danny and persuaded him to take an early train home.

The first thing I did when we got back to London was visit the doctor and explain what I had done, and he ran some tests. To my huge relief he rang a couple of days later to tell me that the baby was unharmed, but he also told me that I had been foolish.

'I thought it was OK after the first trimester,' I said without much conviction.

'It's never safe at any stage of a pregnancy to take an excess of alcohol or drugs,' he replied. 'Even taking painkillers can harm a foetus. At six months you may think you are safe because the baby has formed, but you must remember that its brain is still developing. Believe me, Pearl, you should never, and I mean never, think it's safe to take drugs when pregnant.'

Frankie was born on 5 May 1999. He was the most adorable baby, and to my great relief there was nothing wrong with him. He was a picture of health – unlike his mother. I am not sure what triggered it, because I had been so happy when he first arrived, but within a matter of weeks I was hit by the most terrible blues. I loved Frankie to pieces in my heart of hearts, but I just couldn't cope with motherhood this time round. I just didn't take to it. If he was crying in his cot I would ask Danny or the nanny to tend to him. I found feeding and changing him a strain. It didn't help that I had problems breast-feeding, and I felt like a failure when after two weeks I had to resort to formula. And it didn't make life any easier when Danny left to go on tour again. He would be away, on and off, for the next six months.

I was distraught, and I would lie on my bed crying, paralysed with fear, racked with guilt. Daisy, who had just turned ten, took over my role. She would prepare his bottle, comfort him when he was crying, and change his nappy for me when she got up in the morning. She was my saviour. Of course, I should have gone to the doctor about my depression, but rather than seek professional help I turned once again to drugs to alleviate my pain. The only way I could deal with anything was to get out of my head.

14

Aches And Pains

I relied on heroin to lift my mood throughout those summer months of 1999 when Danny was away on his European tour. Then came the Supergrass gig in Paris in September, when I collapsed on the floor in front of Zoë. After that I promised Danny that I would sort myself out. I recognised that I had a problem, but such was my state of denial about the severity of my addiction that I believed I could get clean on my own. I didn't need to see a doctor, a psychiatrist or a counsellor, and I didn't want to be holed up in some clinic or hospital for that matter either. No, what I needed was a nice little break away from it all, and then I'd stop. A weekend at a spa would do it.

'It will be really good for us,' I told Danny in bed one night as I flicked through the brochure for a luxurious health farm in the country. 'We can have lots of treatments, swim in the pool and take it easy. I'll come back home feeling so healthy and energised I'll never want to take drugs again.' We had been back from Paris for just under a week, and despite everything that had gone on that weekend I was still using. Danny didn't seem to mind, in fact he was my partner in crime. We had spent the best part of the week taking drugs, and he was just as up for it as I was. He was on a six-week break from his tour and he wanted to make the most it.

'Are you sure it's the right thing to do?' he asked. 'You think two days at a health farm is the answer?'

'Of course,' I said, putting down the brochure. 'Come on, it's not like I'm a total junkie! So I take drugs here and there – everyone we know takes drugs. And sometimes I go a bit crazy, but that doesn't mean I have to enrol in some 28-day programme!'

'I guess you're right. Why don't you go ahead and book it.'

The night before Danny and I left for our weekend at the health farm we scored. Well, why not? I might as well go out in style and have a blow-out the night before I settled into a life of abstinence. My mother had taken the children for the weekend so we had the night to ourselves. We never intended to get completely out of it, just a line or two and a smoke, but with Danny and me nothing ever went to plan, and before we knew it dawn was breaking and we hadn't been to bed.

'Do we have to go?' Danny moaned as I packed our bags.

'Yes, we do. It's all booked, paid for and it's costing a small fortune, so we're going. Once you're there being pampered and preened you'll feel so much better,' I said.

By the time we arrived at the health farm we were both feeling extremely fragile. We were hung over, dehydrated and suffering from lack of sleep.

'I can't do this!' Danny groaned as he fell on to our bed. 'You go and have your treatments and I'll just stay here, order room service and have a rest.'

'You can't! I've booked you in for a hot wax wrap and a massage this afternoon.'

'What on earth is a hot wax wrap?'

'I don't know, but I'm sure you'll find it relaxing, and you're bound to fall asleep during the massage. Just enjoy it, that's what we're here for.'

Having changed into a white towelling robe, I left Danny in the room and padded down the hallway to the spa, where I was to have an acupuncture session, some reiki healing and a manicure.

I wanted to make the most of my treatments, and so when the acupuncturist and the reiki healer asked about my health and lifestyle at the beginning of each session I decided to be completely honest with them. Neither baulked when I told them that I had come there because I wanted to get off heroin, in fact they couldn't have been more understanding. The acupuncturist placed extra needles at certain points of my body to help with my withdrawal, whilst the reiki healer worked on relieving me of the tensions that had built up in my body as a result of my drug use. I felt so relaxed by the end of the session that I started to cry. By the time I arrived back at the room later that afternoon I felt invigorated and almost human again. Danny, on the other hand, looked anything but.

He was sitting on the bed in his towelling robe with his head in his hands.

'What's wrong?' I asked. 'Didn't you have a nice afternoon?'

'No, I didn't!' he shouted at me. 'I feel terrible and it's all your fault!'

'What?'

'It's your fault! You did this on purpose, you cow. Do you know how awful that hot wax wrap is? Do you?'

The hot wax wrap had sounded nice when I read about it

in the brochure, but I guess if you were tired, hung over and coming down off heroin and coke it wasn't the best treatment to have. They had wrapped Danny up like a mummy, to the point where he couldn't move, and left him lying there on a bed alone in the dark.

'I thought I was going to die. I couldn't see, I couldn't move. I was itching and sweating. I couldn't breathe. I was screaming for help but no one came. It was hell!'

'What about the massage? That must have made you feel better.'

'That was just as bad, if not worse,' he said accusingly. 'I thought you said the massage would send me to sleep, but I have just spent the last hour having the life knocked out of me by some Thai woman who climbed on to my back, walked all over it and then started yanking my arms and legs out of their sockets.' He pulled down his robe from his shoulders and showed me his back. It was covered in red marks from where she had pummelled and pulled him.

I couldn't help but laugh.

'It's not funny, Pearl! I'm in agony. I hate this place and I hate you for bringing me here. I'm not spending another minute here. I'm going home.'

Within half an hour we were packed and out of there. On the journey home Danny started to see the funny side of his ordeal. 'I'm never going to let you take me anywhere like that again. Health farm indeed! That was more like a torture chamber!'

When we got back to the house it was late evening. I rang my mother to check on the children, but they were asleep so she suggested she kept them until the morning.

'So what do you want to do tonight, now we're at a loose

end?' Danny asked. I knew what I wanted to do; in fact I had already made the arrangements. I had called my dealer as soon as I got off the phone to my mother and he was already on his way over. 'I'll give up tomorrow,' I told myself. But, of course, I didn't.

My problem was that I didn't really want to stop taking drugs. I truly believed that drugs weren't the cause of my troubles but the answer to them. When I was down or depressed I turned to heroin to help me through the dark times. If I was going out and wasn't really in the mood, then a couple of lines of coke would get me going. When I wanted to unwind at night after a stressful day with the children I'd have a smoke. I couldn't really imagine life without drugs, and I refused to accept that they had anything to do with my problems. I convinced myself that I suffered from bouts of depression because I was a creative person and it went with the territory. I believed I was struggling with the children because I was on my own so much of the time. I thought I couldn't sleep at night because I worried too much. I put the dark circles under my eyes down to sleepless nights. I had a litany of excuses at hand to justify my behaviour and mood, for I just couldn't accept that ultimately it was my dependency on drugs that was the real cause of my pain.

Four weeks had passed since we had returned from the health farm and I was beginning to feel incredibly low. When we got back from Paris I had been in high spirits because Danny was around and I felt happy and secure in his company, but our time together was drawing to an end and in a fortnight he would be gone again. I faced another six-week stretch without him and it felt as if I had been condemned to a prison sentence. I just didn't know how I was going to cope without him. I was consumed with fear and dread.

To make matters worse I knew that Danny was getting excited about going off on tour again. Much as he loved taking time off and being at home with the children, he lived for his music. Music was his great passion and his band were his second family and I was starting to resent that. I know it was irrational, for when we first got together this had been one of the things that had attracted me to him, but now I begrudged it. It was all fine and good for him. He could go on tour, do what he loved doing, get paid for it, and still have a loving family to come home to. But what about me? What did I have? I knew I was lucky to have him and the children and our beautiful house, but it always felt as though something was missing, that somehow all that wasn't enough. So long as Danny was around I was OK because he was such a hands-on father, but I knew that once he was out of the door again I wouldn't be able to cope on my own.

The Saturday before Danny was due to go back on tour he had gone off to meet up with the band for a rehearsal and I was alone at home with the children. I wasn't feeling my best that morning as, needless to say, I had been up most of the night using, but I had to take Frankie to the doctor as he had a slight fever. As I didn't have any help at the weekends and couldn't leave the children on their own at home, I took Daisy and Alfie with me. Because it was a Saturday I hadn't been able to make an appointment, so we had to chance it at the surgery and hope that someone could see us. When we got there, however, there was a long queue and I was told that it would be at least an hour before anyone could see us, so I decided to go home and ring for the call-out doctor. It was going to cost me money but I had little choice. I knew I couldn't keep Daisy and Alfie waiting an hour in that surgery. We drove back home, and once I had parked I gave Daisy the door key and asked her to open the front door. I got Alfie out of his car seat and put him in his pushchair, strapped him in and went back to the car to fetch Frankie. My back had been turned for less than a minute when I heard the chair roll off the pavement and into the road. On leaving the kerb the pushchair fell on to its side with Alfie in it. It was then that I realised that I hadn't secured the brake on the chair. I put Frankie down and ran to Alfie. He had hit his head on the pavement and was crying. I screamed for Daisy to come out and help. Having ascertained that he was conscious and that he hadn't cut himself, I lifted the chair up and unstrapped him, and then rushed him into the house and put him down on the sofa. Daisy waited by the car with Frankie, who was also crying by now, until I came out to fetch him.

I rang the call-out doctor immediately and explained what had happened. He was at the house within half an hour and gave Alfie a thorough check-up.

'He's absolutely fine,' he said. 'He's had a slight bang to the head but it's not serious. I think the chair must have protected him. There's no need for him to go to the hospital, he's just had a nasty shock, that's all – as *you* have by the look of things.'

I was in shock, but I was just so relieved that he was fine.

The doctor looked at Frankie and told me to give him some aspirin to bring his fever down. 'Is there anything else you need?' he asked.

'Oh, just the sleeping pills I requested when I called.' I had taken so many sleeping pills over the last few weeks that I was on the verge of running out, and I knew that I couldn't do without them.

'You have your repeat prescription on you?'

'Yes,' I said, fumbling in my bag.

The doctor looked at the prescription and took a bottle from his bag. He then decanted the prescribed amount into a smaller bottle and handed it to me.

'You seem to have a lot on your hands,' he said as he left. 'You should try and relax if you get the chance.'

'I will, I will,' I said. I shut the door behind him and took a deep breath. I couldn't believe that I had been so stupid as not to have put the brake on the chair. It was completely irresponsible of me, and I was just so lucky that he wasn't seriously hurt.

After the doctor left I had to get Frankie settled in his cot for his nap. Once I had done that I went downstairs to check on the others. Daisy had switched the television on and was sitting on the floor happily watching cartoons with Alfie by her side.

'Are you two OK?' I asked.

'Fine,' said Daisy without looking up from the television.

'Good. I'm going upstairs, so if you need me I'll be in my bathroom.'

I grabbed my handbag and went upstairs. I had been planning on dyeing my hair that day, and now that the children were settled this was as good a time as any. I went to the bathroom, got out the hair dye and a roll of tin foil. I looked around the bathroom for some scissors to cut the foil with but there weren't any there, so I headed downstairs again to the kitchen. I got to the hallway of the house and saw Alfie sitting there eating something. At first I couldn't tell what he was munching on, but as I got closer, to my horror, I could see that he had my bottle of sleeping pills in his hand. I realised that I had left them on a table in the hall when the doctor had given them to me, and had forgotten to take them upstairs. But how on earth had he got the cap off the bottle? I knew this wasn't the time for questions. I picked Alfie up from the floor and rushed him to the downstairs loo, where I forced his mouth open and pulled the pills out with my fingers. When his mouth was empty I put my finger down his throat and made him sick, then I reached for the phone and called an ambulance.

'What's going on?' asked Daisy, still glued to the television.

'I have to get Alfie to the doctor.'

'Not again!' was her reply.

As soon as he got my call, Danny left his rehearsal and joined me in A&E at the Royal Free Hospital. Both Daisy and Frankie were with me, as I hadn't had time to arrange for anyone to come and sit with them. Much to my relief, Alfie was OK. I had done the right thing by making him sick and emptying his stomach, but the doctors wanted to give him some coal preparation just to be on the safe side. As we sat there in reception waiting for Alfie to be treated, I began to sob. The events of the last few hours had taken their toll on me and I was overwhelmed with emotion. I had put my child's life in jeopardy not just once that day but twice, and I couldn't forgive myself for that. On top of this I was now beginning to withdraw from the heroin I had taken over the last few days. I was sweating and a sharp pain was drilling through my body.

Danny put his arm round me. 'It's OK, it's OK,' he kept saying.

'It's not OK – he could have died.'

'But he didn't and he's going to be fine. You heard the doctors say you did the right thing – you saved his life.'

'If it wasn't for me he wouldn't have been in that situation in the first place. I'm a terrible mother and I don't deserve to have children!'

We got home later that afternoon and I put Alfie straight to bed. I went down to the kitchen and sat in a heap at the table. Danny looked at me. 'It's not your fault. It really isn't. It was an accident, that's all. I blame the doctor. He can't have put the cap on the bottle properly. How else could Alfie have opened it?'

'It *is* my fault. It's my fault for not taking the pills upstairs. It's my fault for leaving him unsupervised.'

'You can't see it like that.'

'But I do! You don't get it, do you? Alfie is only here because I came downstairs! What was I thinking leaving him alone after what had happened to him earlier? What kind of mother am I?'

'He wasn't on his own, he was with Daisy.'

'Daisy is ten!' I shouted. 'She shouldn't be looking after him. I should be. I'm a useless mother. I can't be trusted to put the brake on his pushchair, to keep pills out my children's reach. I'm an unfit mother!'

Danny tried to comfort me, but nothing he said would assuage the guilt I felt. The children weren't safe in my care, I had proved that.

'You can't go on tour this time, Danny. I just can't do this on my own.'

'But you aren't on your own, you have help, and I'm only going away for six weeks.'

'Six weeks is an eternity to me. And, yes, I have help but only during the week.'

'Then we'll get more help.'

'The way I am at the moment I would need help round the clock – a weekend nanny, a night nurse, a nanny to care for me! Face it, Danny, I can't even look after myself properly, let alone the children.'

He didn't reply.

I knew after that day that something had to give, and I knew what it was. I had to stop taking heroin, I saw that now. 'I'm not doing it again,' I told Danny. 'It's messing up my life. I have to stop once and for all. None of this getting clean and then back on it. It just doesn't work when you've got kids.'

For the first time he agreed. 'Do you want to go to rehab?'

'No, I can do it myself. I know I can.'

Completely oblivious to my drug addiction, my mother believed that I was going through some kind of breakdown. 'It happens to a lot of women after they have a baby,' she told me the next day. 'People get depressed. It doesn't mean you don't love your baby or the other children. It can be purely hormonal. Why don't you see the doctor and try and see if he can give you something to make you feel better? Or maybe you could go somewhere – a clinic or somewhere like that and have a break for a couple of weeks,' she suggested.

'A clinic?'

'Yes, a clinic. There is no need to feel embarrassed about getting professional help. I really think you need to get to the root of your problems, Pearl, if not for yourself then for the children.'

In the days that passed I felt a lot of shame and cried every day. I had failed everyone – Danny, the children, my parents and myself. It didn't help that I was now going through cold turkey. As I withdrew from heroin I suffered from acute mood swings. When I was angry with myself I would take my rage out on Danny and would scream at him for no reason. When I was depressed I would lie on my bed in a catatonic state for hours at a time. I was so weak I could barely move. I felt incredibly limp and suffered from the shakes and cold sweats. One afternoon a friend of mine came round to give me a massage, but I didn't have the strength to climb on to her table, so she had to give it to me in bed instead. As the week went on I became extremely sick. I couldn't hold down my food and was losing a lot of weight. At night I couldn't sleep, yet by day that's all I seemed to do.

I knew that I was doing the right thing by coming off the drugs, but I still couldn't see how I was going to cope without Danny. The whole idea of being on my own, feeling the way I did, filled me with terror. I just didn't want him to leave.

'Are you sure you can't stay?' I would ask him over and over again.

'You know I can't. Look, it's really not that long, you'll be fine. You've got your mother and you can call me any time. You'll get through this, you know you will.'

I wasn't convinced.

The morning Danny left to go on tour I suffered a panic attack. As he started to pack and I realised that he wasn't going to change his mind I became hysterical.

'You can't leave me like this, you can't!' I sobbed from the bed as he filled his bag.

He didn't say anything.

'Danny, please, please don't go, not this time. I can't do this on my own.'

'You can and you will; you're strong,' he said.

'Can't you just cancel it?'

'I've told you again and again that I can't.' He was starting to lose patience with me.

'Can't you just do this for me?'

He stared at me with a look of complete disbelief. 'Are you mad? What do you expect me to do – ring the others and say it's off because you're not feeling so great? This tour has been planned for months.'

'They could get a replacement,' I sniffed. 'They could find someone to take your place.'

Furious, Danny threw down the clothes he was about to pack. 'You just don't get it, do you? I can't stay. I have to go. This is my job! I'm in a band, for God's sake, and that's what we do – go away and tour! You of all people should know that. Who do you think pays for all this? How do you think we live? This is the only way!'

It was clear that any sympathy Danny had felt for me over the past few weeks had gone. My behaviour had pushed him to the edge, and I believe that had it not been for the children he probably would have left me there and then. He'd had his fill of my tantrums and tears, grown tired of my mood swings, my selfishness. This tour offered him a brief respite from the madness and hysteria that had started to plague our lives.

The doorbell rang; it was Danny's car. 'Look, I've got to go,' he said. He came over to the bed and kissed me goodbye. 'You'll be OK and I'll be back soon.' I was crying uncontrollably by now.

'Please, Danny, please stay!' I sobbed. 'Stay this time and I promise I'll make everything all right.'

'You know I can't.' And with that he picked up his bags and left the room.

I prayed that he might have a change of heart on the way downstairs, but when I heard the front door shut behind him I knew he wasn't coming back.

I was distraught and didn't know what to do. I went to the bathroom and took a bottle of sleeping pills from the cupboard. I emptied them into my hand and stuffed them into my mouth, swallowing them with a large glass of water. I went back into the bedroom, lifted the phone and called my mother.

'Mum, it's me,'

'Pearl? What's the matter? What's wrong?'

'I've taken some pills.'

'What pills?'

'Sleeping pills.'

'How many have you taken?'

'I don't know . . . some . . . a lot . . . I don't know . . .'

'How many pills are left in the bottle?'

'Not many.'

'Where's Danny?'

'He's gone.'

My mother came round immediately and let herself into the house. Daisy, Alfie and Frankie were still asleep in their rooms. Having checked on them quickly she rushed up to my room. I was lying slumped on the bed, delirious. Just as I had dealt with Alfie days earlier, my mother lifted me off the bed, got me to the bathroom and made me throw up. Once she was sure my stomach was empty she called the doctor, and after that she rang Danny on his mobile.

'I'm afraid you are going to have to come home,' she said. 'You know I wouldn't do this to you unless it was important, but she's very sick now.'

'But I can't! I have to go on tour. It's too late for me to change my plans.'

'Danny, you are going to have to. I'm afraid it's serious. I think we will have to get her to a clinic – *today*.'

Danny was half-way to Heathrow airport when my mother called. He got his driver to turn off the motorway and head back to Stratford Villas. He rang his band mates and told them that he had to go home. He didn't say why, only that he had to deal with a very serious family issue, but I am sure they must have known what was going on. As they set about trying to find a replacement drummer at a moment's notice, Danny and my mother began to find a clinic for me to go to. It wasn't an easy task. For a start it was a Sunday and they couldn't get hold of our family GP or my health insurance company to see whether I was covered for psychiatric treatment, but after a couple of frantic calls they found a psychiatrist who said she could help.

By taking the sleeping pills I hadn't meant to kill myself, I wouldn't have done that to the children. It was purely and simply a cry for help. And it had worked. Danny was coming back. Five hours later I was admitted to the psychiatric ward of the Charter Nightingale Hospital in London.

15

The Bird House

I checked into the Charter Nightingale, on Lisson Grove, shortly after lunch-time on Sunday, 7 November 1999 to be treated for post-natal depression. Once again my mother stepped into the breach and offered to look after the children whilst Danny drove me to the hospital, but it was decided that it was just too much for her to look after all three of them, so Alfie came with us.

'Where are we going?' Alfie asked from his child seat in the back of the car.

Danny paused, searching for an answer. Realising that he couldn't very well tell his three-year-old son that his mother was about to be checked into the psychiatric unit of a hospital to be treated for mental illness, he told him, in reference to the film *One Flew Over the Cuckoo's Nest*, that I was off to a 'bird house'.

'The bird house? We're going to a bird house!' Alfie was clearly excited by the prospect of an outing. 'Why are we going to a bird house?'

'Because that's where Mummy needs to be right now,' Danny said. 'She has to go and spend a little time with the birds and then she'll come home again.'

'Birds. We're going to see birds!' he kept singing.

Arriving at the hospital, an imposing Victorian building in the heart of Marylebone, we introduced ourselves at reception and were then ushered into a waiting-room whilst my paper-work was completed.

Danny sat there in stony silence.

'Where are the birds, Daddy? Where are the birds, Mummy?' Alfie kept asking us looking round the stark waiting-room. 'I *want* to see birds!'

Danny didn't reply. He just didn't know what to say. He had promised Alfie that we were taking him to see a bird house in an attempt to appease his little boy. But there were no birds here, just a couple of plastic chairs and some very well-worn copies of dreary old magazines. Not knowing what to do, he put Alfie on his knee and stroked his head.

Angry and humiliated, I was overcome with emotion and burst into tears. How could I have ended up here? What was I doing? What kind of a mother was I, putting my child through this?

Danny ignored me. It wasn't out of spite.

Finally a male nurse arrived. 'Miss Lowe,' he said, 'your room is ready for you now. So why don't you say your goodbyes and I'll take you up there?'

I kissed Danny and hugged him and briefly held Alfie in my arms, telling him to be a good boy whilst I was away, but I knew that I had to get out of that room as quickly as possible. I couldn't hold back the tears and I didn't want either of them to see me this way.

When we arrived at my room I have to admit I was appalled. I was well aware that it was a hospital and not a five-star hotel, but I wasn't prepared for this. I had always imagined that these clinics would be more like health farms: large comfy beds, satellite television, spacious bathrooms with towelling dressing-gowns hanging from the back of the door. But this wasn't like the health farm I had visited just weeks before, and it certainly wasn't like the Portland Hospital, where I had been lucky enough to have my children. This was like checking into the most basic suburban B&B, and what was beginning to bother me was that I was well aware that my stay here was costing a small fortune. Fortunately, it was being covered by my health insurance, but I knew just how much a week's stay in this place cost.

The room itself was so tiny that there was only enough room in it for a single bed and a plastic chair pushed against the wall. It was painted beige. The bathroom – if you could call it that – contained a basic shower, loo and basin. On the bed was a slightly shabby looking patterned duvet, on the wall a small television with four channels, and there was no telephone. As soon as I set foot in the room I wanted to get the hell out of there. I can't stay a single night here, I thought, let alone a couple of weeks. Staying here is just going to add to my depression, not alleviate it.

I was told by the nurse to unpack my bags in front of him. As I laid everything out on the bed, each item was checked and listed. Anything that was potentially harmful to me or could compromise my recovery was put on one side. Sharp instruments – such as nail scissors and tweezers – were taken from my wash bag. My mobile phone was confiscated. In the end I was left with nothing more than the clothes I was wearing, some underwear, my pyjamas, hairbrush, toothbrush and paste and a pot of face cream.

Once we had got through that routine the nurse went over

to the door, taking the offending objects with him in a plastic bag. 'Now try and get a little rest,' he said to me sympathetically, as he watched me slump on to the bed, tears still rolling down my cheeks. 'A doctor will come and see you soon.' And with that he shut the door behind him.

But a doctor didn't come. Half an hour passed, then another. By now I was hysterical. What the fuck am I doing here? What is the point? If no one is going to take care of me, then I might as well be at home with my family where I belong. After an hour and a half I got up and made my way to the nurses' station on the ward.

'The doctor hasn't come to see me!' I screamed. 'I thought they said a doctor would come and see me!'

'Oh, I'm sorry, Miss Lowe,' the nurse said patiently. 'It should have been explained to you, but I don't think you will get to see a doctor today.'

'Why not?' I demanded.

'Well, you see, it's a Sunday and we tend to be very short staffed on a Sunday.'

'But I NEED someone to see me NOW. That's why I'm here!'

'I'll see what I can do,' she said, sweetly. 'And I'll try and get someone to bring you some medicine in the meantime.'

'You know, I really shouldn't be in here,' I told her, quite forcibly. 'I really shouldn't. I'm fine. I'm absolutely fine. I'm just a bit tired, that's all.'

'Really?'

'Yes,' I sobbed. 'I'm just a bit tired.'

She smiled at me, with a look that said she had heard all this a thousand times before.

'Can I at least make a call?' I asked. 'I just want to see that my children are all right.'

'Of course, I'm sure that's fine,' she said, handing me the telephone over the desk.

I rang Danny on his mobile. 'Danny, I need to come home, immediately. It's really horrible here and I want to come home and just be with you and the kids.'

At first, Danny just laughed. 'I knew you would ring and say this.'

'But you don't understand, Danny. It's awful. In fact it's worse than awful, it's hell. I don't need to be here. I can't stay a moment more.'

'You can't come home, you know that. I know this is difficult for you, but you have to go through with it. You're there now, so try and make the most of it.'

'I can't. I hate it here. I've made a very big mistake. I just want to come home.'

Although he was trying to be sympathetic I could tell from the tone of his voice that he was beginning to lose patience with me. 'Look, you have to stick this out, you have to get better, not just for you, but for all of us.'

'But no one is trying to get me better. I haven't even seen anyone. I've been alone in my room since you left.'

'Why don't you go and try and mix with some other people?'

'I can't,' I sobbed. 'I promise I'll be fine if I just come home.'

'No! That isn't going to work!' He sounded firm this time, angry even. 'You need help, you need professional help. You need to address this situation.'

Having hung up the phone I went back to my room, my

tail between my legs. I lay on the bed, staring listlessly at the four beige walls, feeling as if I had been condemned to prison. I was scared and I felt horribly alone. A nurse came into the room shortly afterwards and handed me a cup of pills. I gratefully took them from her, gulping them down with a glass of water, and with that I cried myself to sleep.

When I woke the next morning the doctor – my clinical consultant – was already in my room. She was standing at the end of my bed going through my medical charts. She was a tiny Indian woman with a warm and friendly face.

'Well, I think we need to sort you out, don't you? We can't have you feeling like this. We need to make you better.'

There was something so comforting and sweet about her that at once I knew I could trust her. She didn't make me feel ashamed to be there, she didn't make me feel mad, and she didn't seem to judge me either. She treated me as though I was just another patient, suffering from an illness she had yet to diagnose.

'What I would like you to do today, Pearl, is to go to a meeting,' she said.

'What kind of meeting?'

'A group meeting – with a counsellor – so that we can start to get to the bottom of why you are feeling like this.'

I turned my head towards the window. 'I just can't face it today,' I said. 'I'm too depressed. I just want to stay in bed and sleep. I can't face anyone today.'

'OK,' she said. 'If that is how you feel, then that's what you must do. Just stay in bed and rest for now. We can have everything sent to you. Meals will be brought to you, some medication, and you don't have to see anyone, but I am going to ask a therapist to come and visit you when you are feeling a little stronger this afternoon, if that is OK with you?'

'Yes, yes, that would be fine.'

I spent the entire morning in bed, resting. The events of the past week had really taken their toll on me and I was feeling very weak. I also decided that I needed some time and space away from people to reflect on my situation before I spoke to anyone. At around three in the afternoon a counsellor, specialising in depressive illness, came to see me.

'What we need to do first is to get to the core of your depression and discover why and when this started,' he told me. 'Once we have established that it will be easier for us to treat you.'

As he sat on the end of my bed he ran through a long list of questions. We talked about my childhood, my rape, Bonner, my career, my relationship with Danny and the children. As I spoke he made notes.

'So you think this bout of depression began shortly after the birth of your third child?'

'I think so, yes. Well, that's when it seemed to get bad, but I have had periods of depression before.'

'But nothing as severe as this?'

'No, it's never been this bad.'

'OK, Pearl, that's fine. I just want to ask you a few questions about your lifestyle, if that's OK with you? Now what about alcohol? Do you drink?'

'No, I don't drink, I never have done,' I said truthfully. 'I've tried it from time to time but I just don't like it.'

'What about drugs? Do you take drugs – prescription or otherwise?'

I paused, wondering whether to tell him the truth or not. 'Yes, I take drugs, but only, you know, recreationally.'

'What drugs do you take?'

I did not reply straight away.

'Dope, cocaine, heroin? I want you to know that you can be honest with me.'

And so I was. I knew there was no point lying to him. He was there to help.

I had been admitted into the Charter Nightingale ostensibly on the grounds that I was suffering from post-natal depression, but within an hour of that first counselling session I found myself being visited by a drugs therapist. I underwent a series of medical tests. My blood and urine were taken, I was screened for drugs, my blood pressure and heart rate were measured, and I was given a liver function test. After that was completed, we began a very candid discussion about my drug abuse.

Although it was difficult to talk at first, in many ways I found the whole experience incredibly liberating. For the first time in my life I could discuss my drug abuse with a professional, someone who knew what I was talking about, and who was there to help me, not to judge me or cast me aside because I used heroin.

I told the therapist about my addiction. We talked about how often I used. We discussed how I felt when I was on the drug and how I was when I was off it. I told him about what had happened over the last few weeks and what had driven me to stop taking the drug a week ago.

'Well,' he said, putting down his notebook. 'All I can say is this – you are one very lucky lady, Pearl! While I have great admiration for you coming off heroin on your own like you did, I have to tell you that it was also an extremely dangerous thing for you to do. Given the amount of heroin you have been using, most doctors would have insisted that you were put on a course of methadone to ease you off the drug slowly. By withdrawing in the way that you have, you have put your body through quite a lot. You could have died. Your body is extremely depleted and you are not very well at the moment, but I think we can get you right. I'm just very glad you came to us when you did.'

I was immediately put on a very high dose of antidepressants and a series of other medicines that would help me through my withdrawal. 'I'll try you on these for a while,' he told me, 'and then after that, when you have begun to recover, we will lower the dosages. But Pearl, I don't want to just use medicines to treat you, I want you to attend some therapy sessions while you are here as well.'

'Will all this make me feel better?' I asked.

'Yes, you will start to feel better almost immediately,' he told me. 'Within a couple of days your body will start to get back to normal and you will feel much better.'

'Then I'll take it, I'll take anything. I'll go to the meetings even. I just can't go on like this.'

As it turned out, the combination of the antidepressants and the other medicines I was prescribed did make me feel better almost immediately. Within hours I seemed to have regained my energy and was in an upbeat mood. For the first time that day I got out of bed and even made it out of my room. At the nurses' station I asked if I could use the telephone again. They agreed.

'Danny, it's me,' I said. 'I can't tell you how much better

I'm feeling today. These doctors have really sorted me out. I think I'm ready to come home now. Could you come and collect me?'

'Have they said you can be discharged?' he asked.

'Not exactly, but I'm really feeling fine. I really am. I've had a rest and they've put me on some drug to make me feel better, so I really think I'm ready to come back. You know, I feel just great. So much better.'

'You aren't going anywhere!' he scoffed. 'When the doctors give you the all-clear and tell me you are ready to come home I will come and get you, but for now you are staying put.'

Even though the drugs therapist was keen to treat me for my heroin addiction, it was decided by my consultant and the various psychiatric counsellors I saw over the next few days that I should remain on the psychiatric ward rather than move to the hospital's drug rehabilitation unit. Whilst they were aware of the severity of my drug addiction, and accepted that this was contributing to my state of mind, they were still convinced that I was suffering from post-natal depression and believed that this should be tackled first. I was still feeling very fragile and emotional, and they didn't think it was wise to take me off the ward at this stage of my treatment. It was decided that when I was strong enough I should visit the drug unit as a day patient, but for now I would remain in their care.

I would meet on a daily basis with a psychiatrist, as well as attending group therapy sessions. To be honest, I wasn't thrilled by this prospect. Whilst I was happy to attend one-on-one sessions, I didn't want to go to group meetings. My problems were *my* problems – was it really that necessary that I shared them with a group of perfect strangers? Their answer was, simply, yes. Group therapy, in their experience, was one of the most effective cures in the treatment of depression.

I remember my first group therapy session as though it was yesterday. I was led by a nurse to a room not far from the ward. Seated in a circle of plastic chairs were a group of eight people, one of whom was a counsellor. There was just one empty chair left, and I realised that I was the last to arrive. Nervously, I stood in the doorway, unsure of what to do next. I was like a rabbit frozen in the headlights. Sensing my unease, the counsellor bade me into the room.

'Welcome to the meeting,' he said gently. 'Take a seat and then we will begin. Now most of you know the procedure, but for those who don't, what I want you to do as we go round the group is to introduce yourself – first names only are fine – and explain to the rest of us why you are here.' To my profound relief I wasn't the first person to be picked on. Instead, the counsellor turned to a bespectacled man in his mid-forties.

'Hello, my name is Jeremy,' he began. 'And I am here because my wife has left me. Last year she ran off with another man and took our children with her. Since then I haven't seen or heard from her or from them and I feel like my whole life has been torn apart. I feel quite destroyed. I have been here now for two months. My friends and family . . . well, I'm not sure they quite understand the pain that I am going through. Sometimes I am so angry I just can't cope, at other times I feel I am grieving, though I know that is ridiculous because they are all still alive.'

He stopped there, removed his glasses and wiped a tear from

his eye. 'I'm here . . . I suppose . . . because I just don't know what to think any more. I just don't know how to cope.'

The counsellor thanked him and moved on to the girl sitting beside him, who couldn't have been more than nineteen.

'My name is Scarlet,' she whispered. She then paused. Minutes seemed to tick by before she spoke again. 'I have been in and out of clinics now for the past seven years.'

'Scarlet, would you like to share with the group why you are here?'

His question was met with silence.

She looked down at her feet and said nothing.

'Scarlet, do you want to contribute to the meeting today or would you like to stop here?'

She didn't answer. She couldn't. She simply couldn't speak.

'Thank you, Scarlet. We will leave it there for today and maybe we will try again tomorrow if you feel better. OK, let's move on to the next person.'

The girl sitting next to Scarlet was extremely beautiful, with thick, jet-black hair that framed her face. I say she was a girl but later on I learnt, when we became friends, that she was only a couple of months younger than me. The reason why I thought she was so much younger was that during the meeting she sat there clinging on to a teddy bear, like a frightened child. It wasn't clear what her story was, but what was apparent was her deep, deep sadness. She said she just couldn't cope with life. It was all too much for her. She wanted to stay in the clinic because it was the only place in the world that she felt safe. 'I can't face it out there,' she would tell me later. 'I'm better off in here, I know that.'

Then it was my turn.

'My name is Pearl,' I said, 'and I have only been here for a few days.'

My voice was so faint, it was almost inaudible. There was a time, not so long before, when I wouldn't have had a problem performing live in front of thousands of people. Now, I was struggling to introduce myself to a room full of nine.

'Is this your first meeting, Pearl?'

'Yes.'

'Welcome to the group, Pearl. Why don't you tell us why you are here?'

'I don't really know,' I ventured. 'In fact I have no idea what I am doing here,' I said after a pause. 'I just don't know. On the face of it my life is pretty fantastic. I have a lovely boyfriend, three beautiful children, a nice house, no financial worries, everything is great, my life is just great – everyone tells me that. But I'm sad. I'm just really sad.'

'What's making you sad, Pearl?'

'Well, my boyfriend . . . he's in this band, you see . . . and that means he has to go away a lot, and that makes me sad. Recently that has made me really sad, which I guess is why I am here.'

As I spoke and I heard those words spill out of my mouth I realised what a pathetic and selfish cow I was. You sound so spoilt and privileged, I thought. Your partner hasn't left you and taken your children from you. You haven't been so depressed that you have spent most of your adult life in an institution. You aren't so lost in life that you are clutching on to a teddy bear for support. You are loved, you have a life, you have kids. What on earth are you doing talking to these people, these manically depressed, seriously ill people – with real stories and real problems – about your petty little issues? Here you are telling these poor people about your lovely, successful boyfriend, who loves and adores you, your nice house, your beautiful kids, your music career. Why are you sitting there crying? And that was the moment when I knew I had to get my life back. That was my turning-point.

I realised then, for the first time in my life, that my problems were all completely self-inflicted. I had brought all this misery upon myself. And I decided there and then that I had to do something about it. I didn't want to be a victim. I wasn't a victim. I could pull myself out of this and I would. I would get better and I would be out of here. I would do it for myself. I would do it for my children and for my family and friends. And I would do it for the people in this room, people with very real, maybe even unsolvable problems.

I felt humbled being in that group. I realise that pain is pain, no matter who you are. You can't say to someone your troubles are any worse than theirs; life doesn't work like that. It doesn't matter how trivial the source of your pain is – if you feel it, then you feel it. But I realised during that first meeting, when I was talking about Danny and the children and all that I had, that I did have something to live for, I did have a genuine reason to be happy and enjoy life. And I needed to get well to come back to them. I missed them dreadfully and I was determined to go home. I wanted to get back to my life and put it all right.

I am not going to pretend for one moment that it was easy. There were moments that were extremely painful for me. Facing up to my problems, admitting my mistakes – at times it was very difficult. And even though I made friends in the clinic I was still feeling very lonely. Danny came from time to time to visit, but with three children to care for it wasn't that easy for him to get away. When he told me that the boys kept crying for me and that Daisy kept asking when I was going to come home again, my heart broke.

Zoë came to see me during my first week in the hospital, but as soon as she saw me lying in my bed she burst into tears.

'Why are you crying, Zoë?'

'I just can't cope with this. I can't cope with the fact that my best friend thinks her life is so shit she ends up in a clinic. It just isn't right.'

After a week of psychiatric treatment the doctors decided that I should start to attend daily meetings at the drug re-habilitation unit. They still didn't want to move me there on a permanent basis, though, as they were worried that I might relapse in there. There had been a couple of cases that month of people trying to bring drugs into the unit, and they knew I wasn't strong enough to deal with that at this stage.

I was apprehensive about attending rehab meetings. It's one thing knowing privately that you have a problem with drugs, it's quite another admitting it to other people. I was well aware by now that I was addicted to heroin, but it had always been my little secret. Now I was going to have to stand up in front of a whole group of people and admit to it. 'Hello, my name is Pearl, and I'm a drug addict.' The notion of being defined by my addiction made me so ashamed. I wasn't Pearl the singer, Pearl the girlfriend of Danny Goffey, Pearl the mother of three. I was Pearl the heroin addict.

As it turned out, the sessions weren't as bad as I had imagined them to be. The first thing that struck me was just how ordinary the people who attended the meetings were. They were not the stereotypical junkies you see on television – they were normal people with families, jobs, things to live for. They had everything going for them, except for one thing – their addiction to drugs. One mother in the group, whom I befriended, told me that she had become so addicted to crack that her children had been taken away from her by Social Services. She had been told in court that unless she got clean she wouldn't see them again. She's just one step on from where I am, I thought. That could be me if I carry on like this.

I went to the meetings every day. I found it therapeutic listening to other people's stories, and it was helpful to know that I wasn't alone. During one session the counsellor explained to the group how and why people became addicted to drugs.

'First you start taking them recreationally,' he said. 'You do it now and again for a bit of fun. Then you learn to control your drug use, as it becomes a habit. Then one day you cross that line, you reach the point where you can no longer control it, and there you are, a fully-fledged drug addict.'

The consequences of becoming a drug addict were straightforward, he said. 'Once you are a drug addict and you don't do anything about it you have three options. Prison. An Institution. Or Death.' In case any of us hadn't heard what he was saying, he spelt our options out on a blackboard.

I got the message loud and clear.

I began to realise over those sessions just how severe my addiction was. For the first time I understood that by taking heroin I was destroying my life, and it occurred to me just how much I had to lose. It had to stop here. I had to get clean.

I had always had clean times in my life before. Months would go by when I didn't touch drugs, but they were never permanent. I never imagined a life without drugs altogether. But now I was making a conscious decision to stop using once and for all. It wasn't a case of deciding that I *would* never take drugs again, it was the realisation that I *could* never take drugs again. It was that simple.

Once I accepted that, I was actually relieved to be clean and was determined to stay that way. I was on a path and I wasn't going to come off it. I felt happy and strong and I looked forward to my future.

Physically I felt better too. I was sleeping soundly at night and was eating regularly. I was putting on weight and getting my looks back. The circles under my eyes began to fade. I got some colour in my cheeks and the whites of my eyes became clearer, less bloodshot. But the most amazing thing about my physical recovery was that I had no desire for drugs at all. There wasn't one moment, once I started attending the drugs meetings, when I even contemplated the idea of taking drugs. They had lost their allure.

After a fortnight the consultant came to see me. 'You have done very well here, Pearl, and we are all very pleased with the progress you have made,' she said, reading my chart. 'Now, in most people's cases, especially when they have addiction issues, I would recommend that they complete a 28-day programme here as an in-patient. But I understand your situation and know that you have a young family waiting for you at home. How would you feel about coming to see us as an out-patient? Would you like that? Would you like to go home now?'

16

Pink Clouds

I had been warned before I checked out of the Charter Nightingale after my two-week stay that initially I might find it difficult to adjust to life outside the clinic. Whilst I would be the first to admit that a stint in one of those places is by no means a walk in the park, there is no question that within the confines of the hospital one feels safe and secure. It was explained to me that some in-patients found life on the outside extremely daunting, and that there might be times when I felt vulnerable and frightened. In fact I had no such feelings.

When the consultant told me she believed I was ready to go home I couldn't have felt more elated. I couldn't wait to be reunited with my family. I didn't feel scared, I wasn't nervous; on the contrary, I felt extremely empowered and strong. I had not only come round to the idea of living a clean life, I actually liked it. For the first time in many years I felt happy and I wanted to stay that way. Why on earth would I want to jeopardise all that I had achieved for the sake of drugs? I had learnt my lessons, I had got well again, I was on my path and no one, nothing, was going to tempt me off it.

Danny came to collect me from the hospital, and as we arrived back at the house, my family – Daisy, Alfie and Frankie and my parents – were waiting for me. All the people I loved most in the world were around me. As I walked through the door into the house it felt as though I had been released from prison – although what I had come to realise during my treatment was that my prison hadn't been my stay in the clinic but my addiction to drugs. I understood that now. And here I was, free at last.

From now on everything would be different. Everything would change. It was a new beginning for all of us and I was excited about that. I wanted to put everything right and make up for all the damage and the destruction I had caused over the years through my own selfishness. I would no longer be an absent mother, girlfriend, daughter or friend. I would no longer put myself before others or take my loved ones for granted. I wouldn't allow my addiction to drive a wedge between my family and me. I would no longer let heroin dictate my life. I would no longer be a junkie.

To help myself make a fresh start, one of the first things I did when I returned home was to redecorate my bedroom. To some that might sound frivolous, but for me it was an extremely important psychological exercise. For many years that room had been the scene of so much of my drug-taking. I would spend hours locked in that squalid den, with its walls painted the colour of smack, lying on my bed smoking heroin and drifting in and out of consciousness. I no longer wanted to live with those associations. I didn't want to be surrounded by physical reminders of my past, and so within a matter of days I transformed it into a wonderful, pure, clean sanctuary by painting it a brilliant white.

The second thing I did when I got home was to book a

holiday in the Caribbean for the whole family, including my parents. I thought we could all do with a couple of weeks in paradise, and I wanted to spend some quality time with my family. I owed it to them. So it was arranged that shortly after a quiet family Christmas, which we would celebrate on our own at home, we would head to the island of St Lucia to see in the new millennium.

I reinvented myself as a mother, now devoting all my time to the children. I spent hours playing with Daisy and Alfie. We would lie on the sofa and watch television together in the early evening. There were bedtime stories and games, and regular trips to the park. I took them on special treats and always made sure that I was the one who collected them from school. Daisy and Alfie were thrilled to have me back, and as for Frankie, well, just looking at my baby son, so vulnerable and small, I couldn't believe that I had neglected him all those months. He was the most adorable, well-behaved, good-natured child, and I hated leaving him now, even for a couple of hours.

Now that I was off the heroin and no longer spending half my life in the bathroom being sick, I rediscovered my appetite and my love for cooking. There were regular family meals and always a big roast at the weekend. When December came I threw a huge Christmas party for the children. In the past I would have used this as a good excuse to throw a party of my own, ordering in cases of wine and inviting my friends, regardless of whether they had children or not. But this time it was different. I made cakes, baked biscuits and arranged party games for the children to play. I spent hours decorating the house, transforming it into a Winter Wonderland. And this time I invited all *their* friends rather than my own; this was their party, not mine.

Heroin 'chic'. I cringe now when I look at this photo.

This was taken on a photo shoot for Lodger.
Daisy came along too.

Me and Zoë on a tour bus at V Festival

Danny, Daisy and me in a photo for *Select* magazine. I was pregnant with Alfie at the time. Why was I wearing *moonboots*?

Me and the boys from Lodger.

My life was a rollercoaster of ups and downs. When I was clean and spending time with Danny and the kids, everything was great.

But when I was 'being Pearl' - singer, party girl - as I was here at Danny's 30th birthday party, my life was a disaster.

This photo of Daisy and me makes me sad now - I look so gaunt. I was using more than ever.

A solo gig at
Ronnie Scott's.
I got wasted and
blew it.

Pearl
plus mankato

Ronnie Scott's
47 Frith Street, Soho, W.1.
Sunday 22nd February, Doors 7.30

Tickets £10 Advance (£12 Door) Box Office 020 7439 0747
Credit Cards 08700 600100 Online at www.ticketweb.co.uk

ronnie
scott's
OPEN NIGHTLY

Only £10 with flyer on the door.

I love this photo of
Danny and me.

Pregnant with Betty, living in the country and content for the first time in years.

Rhys Ifans has been a great friend over the years.

Carl Barat and me at a fundraiser for the homelessness charity, Crisis, that I helped to organise.

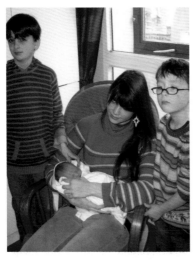

My beautiful babies, Daisy, Alfie, Frankie and Betty. These days I live for them.

Baby Betty!

I'm so proud of Daisy.

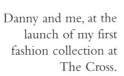

Danny and me, at the launch of my first fashion collection at The Cross.

Danny was amazed by my metamorphosis. For him it was like living with a different person. No longer the listless junkie who put her wants and desires before his, I was now bursting with energy and had a zest for life. He was able to get back to work, which was a great relief to him, and was just thrilled that I was better and happy. There were no more tears through the night, no hysterics when he left to perform at a gig or went away on tour, no more fights and dramas. There was nothing for him to worry about. I was his girl again.

When I left the clinic I had been advised by a psychologist that I should be very wary about who I mixed with now that I was clean. It is a message that they give to all recovering addicts no matter what your poison is. Tear up your address book, clear your SIM card, change your playmates and your playground. Avoid the people that will lead you into temptation, the ones who aren't clean. Move house if necessary, just try to stay away from your old life if you want to stay on the path to recovery.

For the first few months I was clean this was easy for me. All I really wanted was to spend time with Danny and the children. I had no intention of going out at night, and I wasn't interested in parties. I was happy for Danny to go out and hang out with his friends if he wanted to, but I no longer wished to come along for the ride. I wanted to be at home where I belonged. I spent a lot of time with Zoë during those months, which was wonderful. When I was using, even though she was my best friend, I would go for weeks without calling her, either fearful that she might realise I was on smack or simply because I was too high or too low to stay in contact. But now we spoke every day. A contributing factor to this was the fact that Zoë had decided to clean up her own life as well. Although she had never suffered from drug addiction, Zoë did like to drink, but after she visited me in the clinic that evening she had been so shocked and frightened by what had become of me that she made a promise to herself to get sober, and from that night on she never drank again. Having a close friend around me who was clean was really important for me. We helped each other through the dark days and enjoyed being together through the light ones. In the past we would have seen each other nocturnally, as we burnt our candles at both ends, but now we spent our days together, chatting round the kitchen table, drinking tea, happily watching our sons Alfie and Marley, who were the same age, play together.

As for my other friends – the ones I had used with – I spoke to them from time to time on the telephone but didn't see much of them. This wasn't just my decision but theirs too – when you are taking drugs and having a wild time the last thing you want to do is hang out with someone who is clean. What's the fun in that, after all? They know you aren't going to be the life and soul of the party, and they certainly don't want you to cast a shadow on their own. In any case we were now living in different time zones. As their day was coming to an end, mine was just beginning. These days I was up with the larks, no longer going to bed with them.

And so this is how it was for the first few months of my recovery. I still visited the hospital and I attended weekly Narcotics Anonymous meetings, which I found helpful to begin with. I liked the security of being surrounded by a group of people who were all in the same boat as I was. We would talk through our problems, worries and fears and I felt safe there.

When I left the clinic I had been assigned a wonderful drugs counsellor called Paul, and we met twice a week for a one-on-one session. I was very lucky to have met him. He was a very understanding, sympathetic and wise person, who was sensitive to my situation and my needs, and within just a couple of sessions with him he became my rock. I could talk to him about everything and nothing. I could tell him about my fears, re-live my worst periods and question him on anything. He didn't judge me. He didn't lecture me. He simply listened.

Although I had a wonderful relationship with Danny at this stage, and have always considered him to be my closest friend in the world, there were some things I just couldn't talk to him about. Sometimes it is easier to confide in a stranger than the person who is closest to you. And by that stage I had gone through quite a lot. I had done a great deal of soul-searching in the clinic, and I had discovered things about myself that I was still having to come to terms with and wasn't ready to share with the man I loved and who I wanted to go on loving me. On top of all this, I was aware of how much support Danny had given me during the past few months. Not only had he cancelled going on tour whilst I was in the clinic, and been left, quite literally, holding the baby – and the other two children – but when I came home he had been behind me every step of the way. I didn't think it was right, after all he had done, to burden him with anything else.

But with Paul it was very different. He was there to help, that was his job, and, as soon became clear to me, it was also his personal mission. He didn't want me to fall, to go back to my old ways – he really wanted me to stay clean. Sometimes during those sessions we would sit and talk about drugs; on other occasions it would just be about life in general. He put me at ease, made me feel comfortable, even when we discussed some of the more harrowing elements of my drug abuse. He understood the intense shame I felt about my past, and the guilt which overwhelmed me when I thought of my behaviour and the impact it had had on my family and friends. We had long discussions about addiction, and what it was and meant to be an addict. He explained that it was a disease, a self-inflicted disease, and whilst there was no cure for it as such, he made me understand that I could recover from it. He gave me hope. He understood my highs and lows and my depression. He knew when I was having a good day and when I was struggling through a bad one. He even took the time out to talk to Danny, explaining the difference between his recreational drug use and my very dangerous addiction to narcotics. Danny was still using drugs, and he still drank, but only very occasionally and never in front of me. He kept that world away from me, allowing me to stay on my path.

I took my journey very seriously. From time to time I had my difficult days, of course. On Millennium Eve, in St Lucia, when everyone else in the world seemed to be partying and celebrating, I had to take myself off to bed at 9 p.m., knowing that I couldn't be around the ensuing revelries. There were occasions when Danny and I would have to go out at night, because it was someone's birthday or he had a work commitment, and I found these nights difficult to cope with. I would always be fine at first. I quite enjoyed the whole ritual of going out: getting dressed, putting on my make-up and so on. It was good to see people again and catch up. Everyone would tell me how well I looked, which was true. I had put on weight and lost the dark shadows from beneath my eyes, and my skin for the first time in many years glowed. And everyone would tell me how nice it was to see me again. 'Where have you been hiding, Pearl?' they would say.

But come 10 p.m., when the drinks started flowing, the party began to get in full swing and everyone was beginning to get slightly out of it, I knew that it was time for me to make my excuses and leave. I would begin to wane. I knew that I couldn't stick around, because I knew my place and that was at home in my bed.

But for the most part I felt good about myself. In many ways being clean wasn't the struggle that I had always imagined it to be. I didn't miss the drugs. I didn't miss being out of it. I didn't miss being high and I certainly didn't miss coming down, being low and feeling so ill. I began to revel in my new way of life and would extol the virtues of being clean to anyone who would listen. I had reclaimed my life and was proud of that. Our house was no longer the den of iniquity it once had been; it was a home, a family home, and I made sure it stayed that way. People would come for meals and to see us, but there were no late-night parties. I had been a smoker when I was using drugs, but when I got clean I gave that up as well. Smoking – and by that I mean cigarettes, not just heroin – was now banned from the house. If someone wanted a cigarette then they would have to smoke outside. Even Danny had to stand on the doorstep if he wanted to light up. 'It's not good for the children,' I would say in a matronly tone.

I began to see that there was so much more to life than drugs, which was something I had never considered before. I had always imagined that life *was* drugs. To be enlightened, to reach that higher point of understanding and spirituality, to have fun and enjoy life, to live it to the full, then you had to be on drugs. On drugs life was better, richer, more amusing, more pleasurable, or so I thought at the time. Now that I was clean I started taking pleasure in other things. Reading a good book, eating a delicious meal, watching my children learn something new – all these things made me happy, far happier than I had ever felt being high. I didn't need drugs. I didn't need anything more from life than what I had right now – my health, my happiness, my children and Danny. For the first time in my life I felt contented.

Initially, when I came out of the clinic, I had no intention of going back to work. As far as I was concerned that part of my life was over, and as I was lucky enough not to need the extra income, I decided to end Lodger. We had finally finished our album *A Walk in the Park* and released it in January 2000. It had been well received, but I felt we had gone the distance and we shouldn't take it any further. In any case I was enjoying my new incarnation as a 'Stepford wife' and didn't want to spend any more time away from my family than was completely necessary.

I was walking round Primrose Hill one morning with Frankie in his pram, taking him for his daily jaunt round the park, when I bumped into Alan McGee. Alan, at the time, was one of the biggest names in the music industry, having discovered groups like The Jesus and Mary Chain and Oasis, and I had known him for some time. We started talking and he asked me what I was up to.

'Nothing, other than looking after Danny and the kids,' I told him. 'I've given up music for good.'

'You've what?'

'I've given it all up. I'm not interested in going back into the industry. It's just not for me any more.'

He looked incredulous. 'You can't, you can't give up!'

'Why not?'

'Because you are a rock and roll girl. You should be out there.'

'You know, Alan, I just can't be bothered any more.'

'Well you should be bothered. Do you know how few girls like you there are in the industry at the moment? You can't just turn your back on it all, not now.'

He paused for a moment, then suddenly said, 'I'll sign you!'

'What?'

'I'll sign you! I've got a new label out and I'll sign you! What do you say?'

Now had this been anyone else in the industry I would have said 'no', a polite but firm 'no'. But here I was in front of Alan McGee, one of the greatest music moguls around, who wanted to sign me. I just couldn't believe it.

'OK,' I said. 'OK . . .'

I had to wait until the afternoon to call Danny because he was in America, back on tour with the band. 'You won't believe what happened to me today!' I said.

'Tell me,' he said groggily, as he woke, imagining some tale about the children or what new recipe I had tried the night before.

'I've just signed up with Alan McGee!'

'What?'

'Alan McGee. I met him today and he wants me to sign with his new label, Poptones.'

'You have to be kidding.'

'I'm not, I'm totally serious.'

'But baby, you don't have any songs!'

'Well I'll write some – we can write some.'

And so when Danny returned from the States that's exactly what we did. With £30,000 in our hands thanks to Poptones, Danny and I sat down and wrote a beautiful and amazing album together. It was about my addiction to heroin, and I called it *Aches and Pains*.

17

All Cleaned Out

On 7 April 2000, six months to the day after I got clean, I relapsed. It was the night of my birthday, and to celebrate it Danny had thrown me a fabulous party at a private members' club in Soho. I had been in two minds about the party from the start. On the whole I had avoided going out since I was discharged from the clinic. I knew that it was better for me to remove myself from any situation that could compromise my recovery in any way. And in any case I wasn't really in the party spirit. Since I got clean I wasn't interested in socialising, it no longer held any allure for me. I was happiest at home with my family. I got my kicks elsewhere these days: spending time with the kids, cooking Danny dinner, writing songs. I did not need to go out to prove to the world that I was having fun.

I was tempted not to celebrate my birthday at all and just let the day quietly pass me by, but Danny had insisted that we mark the occasion. 'Come on, it will be fun,' he said. 'You deserve it. I'm so proud that you've got this far, I think we should celebrate. You can't go on hiding for ever, you need to get out there.' I thought long and hard about what he said. I couldn't go on shielding myself from our friends; eventually

I would have to start seeing people again. I had come a long way in my recovery, and I was a different person, a stronger one. The time had come for me to face the world, even if it was for one night only.

When I walked through the door of the club that night it seemed as though Danny had invited everyone we knew to the party. There were hundreds of people there and they all seemed to be having a good time. I was glad that Danny had talked me round and was deeply touched that he had gone to so much effort to make this night special for me. I liked seeing my friends again and catching up with them, and I was pleased that so many of them had made it. My one great fear when I had got clean was that I would never have fun again. I couldn't imagine life sober, especially being at a party and not getting slightly out of it, but here I was enjoying myself. It was a whole new experience for me.

As the party went on my mood became more buoyant and I felt on top of the world. After a couple of hours, though, as my guests got merrier and merrier I found myself starting to lag. Danny was on flying form. When I first came out of the clinic he had been very sensitive and considerate about not getting out of it when he was with me. I knew that he drank and that he dabbled in drugs when he was on tour, and I didn't begrudge him that at all. So long as he didn't bring it home with him, so long as he wasn't drunk or high in my company, I was OK, but tonight he was letting his hair down. At the beginning of the evening he asked me whether I minded. 'Not at all,' I answered truthfully. 'All I want is for you to have a good time.'

Another hour passed and I was beginning to feel slightly out of place, as though I didn't belong, even though it was my party. I seemed to be the only sober person in the room now, and it was a lonely place to be. I went to the ladies' loo to freshen up and was standing in front of the sinks, reapplying my lipstick, when one of the cubicle doors burst open and out spilled two of my girlfriends, giggling in a conspiratorial way. 'Pearl!' they shrieked when they saw me standing there. 'We didn't know you were there; come and have a line.'

'That's kind of you, but I think I'll pass,' I said.

'Oh come on! It's your birthday!'

I had meant to say 'no', meant to exert some self-restraint, but before I knew it we had all squashed into the cubicle. 'What the hell!' I thought as my friend cut out the cocaine on the top of the loo seat. 'It *is* my birthday. One line won't hurt, one small line to get me going, then I'll stop.' As anyone who has ever taken the drug knows, one line is never enough. Such is the nature of cocaine that as soon as you have had your first taste of it you just want more and more. Your desire and perceived need for the drug become insatiable. I carried on using coke through the night, and when we got back home with a group of friends in the early hours of the morning, behind Danny's back I smoked a small amount of heroin that had been surreptitiously given me by one of our gang.

At the time I didn't think I was doing anything wrong, because I was too high to know any better, but when I woke the following day and realised the implications of my actions I was filled with self-loathing. I hated myself for being so weak, for giving in to temptation so easily. It was as though all the work I had done in the past six months had counted for nothing. It was like a game of snakes and ladders. I had slowly been working my way to the top of the board when, with one roll of the dice, I suddenly found myself sliding all the way back to the bottom: back to square one.

I should have gone straight to an NA meeting that day – that was what they were there for, after all – but I couldn't face it. I found it too painful to put my hands up and admit my mistake. I had made a lot of friends in that group and had felt I had been on a journey to recovery with them. I had pledged myself to a life of sobriety and they had promised to support me on that road; now that I had fallen I had not only let myself down but them as well. I didn't want them to think less of me because I had stumbled at my first hurdle.

If Paul had been around I would have contacted him, but sadly he had left the Charter Nightingale two months earlier and I didn't know how to get hold of him. I had been appointed a new counsellor but we hadn't clicked. He had all the right qualifications, but I didn't have the same rapport with him that I had enjoyed with Paul. I found him to be judgemental, at times even patronising. And so I rather naïvely decided to take matters into my own hands. I simply made a promise to myself that I would never take heroin again. Even though I had enjoyed the way it made me feel the night before, I knew that I just couldn't go there. I didn't want to live that life; I didn't want to feel ill or have to put myself through cold turkey again.

In retrospect, I am not really surprised that I relapsed when I did. Like many addicts who go through recovery for the first time, I thought that I was 'cured'. I didn't see recovery as an ongoing battle that you have to fight until your dying day, I believed that once you had got on your path there was no turning back. In fact they say that your 'pink cloud' only lasts for three to four months. Once that honeymoon period with sobriety ends, once you get over the novelty of being clean, it's easy to tire of your new existence and to allow your old behavioural patterns to start to set in. That was certainly true of me. I had enjoyed being clean to start with, I had found it empowering, but as the months went on I was beginning to get slightly bored by the predictability of my life. I seemed to be following the same routine every day, and instead of getting a sense of security from it, at times I found it claustrophobic. That's when I should have leant on my network of support more heavily, but because I had so much clean time behind me I misguidedly thought that I didn't need to. I had got through the worst of it, I had learnt all the lessons I needed to know, I could go it alone now. I had got clean and stayed clean, and I hadn't found it that hard. But what I hadn't factored into the equation at that point was that during those first few months I had lived the life of a hermit, cocooning myself at home. I hadn't given in to temptation, but then there hadn't been any around.

I managed to stay clean in the weeks that followed my party, but it was a struggle for I had rediscovered both my taste and my appetite for drugs. I momentarily toyed with the idea of going back to NA, but I still didn't want anyone to know that I had relapsed, and I knew that if I started attending sessions again I would have to stay clean, and I wasn't sure that was what I really wanted. I knew that I wouldn't touch heroin again, but maybe I could indulge in the odd line of coke from time to time – if it was a special occasion, for example. The fact that I had been hooked on heroin didn't necessarily mean that I had to give up *everything*. If I just used in moderation that would be fine. I felt somewhat relieved by my decision, as though a weight had been lifted from my shoulders. When I told Danny he didn't seem that concerned. I had presented a convincing case to him, and to myself; it had been heroin I had been addicted to, not coke, and I would keep my future use of the drug to a minimum. In some ways I think that Danny was secretly pleased that I had come to this conclusion. He liked having fun and living it up, and I know that he was finding it difficult to adjust to my new regime of retiring to bed every night at 9 p.m. with a good book and a cup of tea.

As it turned out I didn't wait for a special occasion to arise before I took coke again. I did it just a couple of days later when we were out together with a group of friends. And I didn't confine my intake to a couple of lines either. I used quite heavily that night. I was, of course, fooling myself that I could keep my use of cocaine under control; all I was doing was swapping one drug for another, but I wouldn't admit it. Because I could go for days without taking it, weeks even, I lived under the delusion that I had my use in check, and because I had clean time behind me I believed that just as I had been able to stop using before, I could do so again. It was an absurd rationale, which went against everything I had been taught in recovery. I had been told numerous times that you didn't have to use every day to classify as an addict, and that addiction stayed with you for life. They had warned me that as an addict I would never be able to take or leave drugs either – I had to avoid them at all costs – but I chose not to dwell on those lessons. Because so many people we knew seemed to use cocaine I liked to think that this made it somehow OK, as though it was no different from drinking wine or spirits or smoking grass. Its use was so socially acceptable that in my mind I declassified the drug from an A to a B. Coke wasn't like heroin: it wasn't physically addictive, it was nothing more than a party drug. I truly believed I could control my use of cocaine and confine it to the odd occasion, and at first I stuck to my word. Within just a couple of months, however, these sporadic sessions had become increasingly frequent and my interludes of clean time were getting few and far between.

'Are you OK, Pearl?' people would ask when I was high on coke. 'Are you sure you're all right?' Unlike other people I knew who used the drug, I never had much fun on cocaine. It didn't make me feel lively or happy, or as if I was about to conquer the world, and it didn't make me confident or chatty either. I was fine after a couple of lines, but if I took any more than that my evening was effectively over. I would get so charged on the drug that I couldn't speak, couldn't think even; the most I could manage was a strained smile. I felt morose, and rather than embrace the party spirit I would withdraw into my own little world.

'You've overdone it again, haven't you?' Danny would say with a sigh, when he found me sitting on my own in the corner of the room, unable to join or even follow the simplest of conversations. My eyes would have widened to the size of saucers, which is why I was given the nickname Gollum, my face would be contorted and my mouth fixed into a peculiar, fish-like pout. 'I wish you'd learn to limit yourself,' he'd say. But I never did, of course. Despite knowing the damaging effects the drug had on me, I would take as much as the next person, if not more.

It didn't take long for me to become hooked on cocaine.

I had promised after my birthday only to take the drug when the occasion was right, when there was a big night out or we were going to a party, but now I was finding any excuse in the book to use it. I made sure that my diary was full, that we went out most nights, simply so that I could indulge, and if there was nothing going on then I would invite people round to the house and stage our own parties. Just as I had my heroin buddies before I went into rehab, I now immersed myself in a group of people who took cocaine on a regular basis and could thus enable my habit. I dropped many of my old friends and had no time for anyone who was clean. I just wanted to be with people who used: people who didn't take drugs were in my mind boring.

I was taking the drug nearly every day of the week and would invariably consume as much as ten or twenty lines in one session. I took it as I was putting on my make-up before we went out in the evening, and even when I was out having lunch with my girlfriends. I'd take a line before we sat down for dinner at a restaurant and would then spend the rest of the evening pushing food around my plate because I was no longer hungry. I tried to ensure that I always had my own coke on me wherever I went, and in case I did find myself running short, I made sure that I had the number of a dealer to call on.

Danny knew that I overdid it when it came to coke, but he wasn't aware of how often I used, as he was on tour for much of this period. Just as I had managed to conceal my heroin habit from him, I kept secret the true extent of my dependency on cocaine. As far as he was concerned I only took the drug when we were together or if I was partying.

He didn't know about the grams of coke I would regularly buy when he was away, the extra lines I would sneak at a party when he was out of sight, or the ones I did during the day. He simply thought that I was using recreationally, as he was. Of course, by lying to Danny, I was in effect lying to myself. Although I knew I had a problem with coke, I didn't accept that it was quite as bad as it was, and as long as I moved within my circle of friends I could convince myself that I was OK, for they always seemed to be using. But within the space of a year my use of cocaine had spiralled out of control. I couldn't keep a lid on it, I believed that I couldn't function without it and, at the risk of this sounding like a bad pun, I never knew when to draw the line.

In the summer of 2001 I was admitted to hospital for an operation. My annual smear test had revealed that I had pre-cancerous cells within the lining of my womb, and I was to undergo laser surgery to have them removed. As the procedure was fairly straightforward I was admitted to the hospital as a day patient, but I was advised that once I was home I would need to get some rest and take it easy for a couple of days. When I returned to the house in the early afternoon there was a message on our answer machine: 'Dinner tonight at the Ivy, 9 p.m. Call back if you can come.'

I didn't have to even think about it. Dinner at the Ivy – how could I refuse?

'Are you sure you should be going out tonight?' was Danny's response when I called him on his mobile to inform him of our date.

'Yes, why not?'

'But I thought the doctor told you to get some rest.'

'Oh, come on. It's not like I've had heart surgery, women have this kind of thing done every day of the week. I'll have a rest now and then I'll be fine. It's only dinner after all.'

Danny was busy in the studio, so we agreed to meet at the restaurant when he had finished.

When I arrived at the Ivy shortly after 9.30 my friends had already gathered at the table. I had been looking forward to my night out, but before we had even ordered our food I became conscious of the fact that I wasn't on form. The others had been tucking into cocktails and wine before I arrived and were already in a raucous mood. I wanted to be on their level, but I knew that I wouldn't get there unless I took some coke. For once, however, I didn't have any on me; nor did anyone else.

'Shall I get some in then?' I volunteered. I knew that I couldn't get my dealer to drop in to the Ivy to make the exchange, so I decided to visit him instead, even though he was based in the East End. Luckily one of my friends had a driver waiting outside the restaurant, so I didn't have to take a taxi. When I got to my dealer's flat he insisted that I come and stay for a while. He didn't like people just popping in and out – it attracted the wrong kind of attention, he explained.

After we made the transaction he gestured for me to sit down. 'Want to try it?'

'Sure,' I said. I felt slightly awkward sitting there, but was thankful he was offering me some drugs. From a mound of cocaine on the glass coffee-table he cut four very generous lines, far wider and longer than anything I would have drawn if it had been my own supply. With my banknote already rolled, I bent over the table and snorted the first. Having hoovered the coke from the table I put my head slightly back and inhaled further so I could feel the full effect of the hit. The drug hit my sinuses and trickled down the back of my throat. I swallowed.

There was no question about it, this was top gear, well worth the journey.

'You like it?'

I nodded. 'Its great!'

'Well have another one then,' he said as he rolled himself a joint.

By the time I got back to the car fifteen minutes later I was flying. I was chatting away to the driver, making no sense, and openly taking drugs in front of him. He didn't seem to care. He had seen all this before. He was used to his clients taking coke and smoking dope in front of him; he was used to waiting outside estates while we scored. Whether he inwardly disapproved or not I will never know, for he just got on with his job and never remarked on it. We drew up outside the Ivy, and I was just climbing out of the car when I noticed that there was blood on my seat, on the white leather interior. I felt my dress, which luckily for me was black, and it was wet where I had been sitting. Without telling him why, I asked the driver if he had a cloth. He reached into the dashboard and passed me a box of tissues. I quickly wiped the blood from the seat and stuffed the dirty tissues into my handbag.

When I got to the restaurant I went straight to the loo. To my alarm I was haemorrhaging. I had been warned that this could happen, and fortunately I had a sanitary towel in my bag. In the back of my mind I knew that I should probably go home and call a doctor, but I didn't want to do that. I wanted to stay out. I had gone out of my way to go and score in order that I could have a good time. I was damned if I was going to leave.

When I got back to the table my friends were in high spirits. Even though I had been gone for over an hour no one seemed to have noticed.

'Been on the phone?' one of them asked.

'No, I went out to score.'

'You're kidding! You are such a star,' said another, kissing me. 'You really are my best friend.'

With most of the party fuelled up on cocaine, it was decided that we should get the bill and make our way to a party in Portland Place.

Danny had just arrived. 'Are you sure you're up to it?' he asked.

'Yes, I'm fine,' I lied.

By the time we got there I was starting to feel very out of it. I was unsteady on my feet and my head was spinning. I went and sat down on a sofa next to my friend. Sean Pertwee. He was in the middle of a conversation with his wife Jackie when I suddenly interrupted them.

'I'm haemorrhaging,' I told them, as if it was the most natural thing in the world to say.

'What?!' He looked at me with disbelief. Both Sean and Jackie were completely sober, and I could tell that they were shocked by the state I was in.

'I'm haemorrhaging. I went to the hospital today and had an operation, and now I'm bleeding.'

'What the fuck are you doing here, then? Are you out of your mind?' Sean said. What I have always loved most about Sean is that out of all my friends he is the one who always speaks his mind. 'Where the hell is Danny?'

'I've no idea.'

'Well, I'm going to find him. In the meantime here's my phone – I want you to call for an ambulance.'

'But I don't want to go, I want to stay!'

'Pearl, you have to go – you have to get seen to!'

Sean found Danny. 'Take Pearl home now! She isn't well.'

'But she said she was fine.'

'She's not fine! She's out of her head and she's haemorrhaging. You need to get her out of here.'

Danny managed to get me home, but I refused to go to a hospital that night because I didn't want them to know that I had taken cocaine. Instead I went to bed. When I woke in the morning the bedclothes were drenched in blood.

'That's it,' Danny said. 'I don't care what you say, I'm taking you to hospital.'

The doctor who examined me was horrified. 'I'm going to have to keep you in for the day, you have lost a lot of blood. Why didn't you come to us last night?'

'I don't know,' I said. 'I just didn't think it was particularly serious.'

'Can you let us be the judge of that in future? Do you realise that you could have died?'

I'm not sure whether I was still out of it, but when he told me that I just laughed. For some sick reason I thought it was funny.

18

Good To Go

*O*n the face of it I'm smiling. Well, why wouldn't I be? My life's great, just great. That's what they all keep saying, keep telling me as they help themselves to yet another glass of champagne, another line of coke during a late-night session at our house in Willesden.

'You've got it all, haven't you, Pearl?' they say.

As far as they are concerned, I have. Of course I have. I have the rock star boyfriend, the seemingly great career and three adorable children. I've got no financial worries, plenty of friends and a beautiful new seven-bedroom home. So why then am I crying inside? Why can't I just stop crying? Why? Why am I so unhappy? Why do I feel like I want it all to stop right here? Why do I go to bed each night feeling as if my life is over? That's what I want to know.

Although I didn't acknowledge it at the time, by the summer of 2001 I was suffering from severe depression. I spent most nights in tears, and would cry into my pillow until morning came. I found it difficult to lift myself out of bed during the day and would lie there for hours in a catatonic state. My energy levels were so low, my concentration was so poor, that completing the simplest of chores defeated me. Even though

I had so much going for me I could derive little pleasure from any of it. Much as I loved Danny and the children, even they couldn't raise my spirits. It was as though all the joy in my life had disappeared. I suppose I should have recognised the signs, having been diagnosed with post-natal depression at the Charter Nightingale and sought professional help, but I didn't. I just carried on operating to the best of my ability, like a half person, a shell. Everywhere I looked there was darkness. I walked under a cloud of gloom and couldn't escape the shadows that seemed to follow me around. I was haunted by negative thoughts, plagued with anxiety, fearful of the future, uncomfortable about my past.

Other than Danny, few people knew how low I really was, and I wanted it to stay that way. I continued to party, to take drugs – which, of course, just perpetuated my depression – and put a brave face on it all. I didn't want people to know what was going on, for then I would have to explain, and I wasn't ready for that. If they wanted to buy into the myth that my life was so bloody perfect, then let them, but that's all it was – a myth – for by the middle of that year I was effectively in freefall. Nothing seemed to be going right for me any more, everything I touched seemed to turn to stone. I was starting to lose my hold on everything that I cherished and had worked for, both personally and professionally.

My career, for example, was all but over. Towards the end of 2000, on a drug-infused whim, I decided that I no longer wanted to be with Alan McGee. Despite the fact that one of the biggest names in the music industry had invested both faith and money in me, I thought I could do better than that and was determined to sign with a bigger label. Alan had been remarkably good-natured about my decision. 'OK,' he said, when I broke the news to him. 'Just give me back your advance when you get your new deal.'

'Fine,' I said, confident that this wouldn't be a problem. But it was, for no one wanted to sign me, no one was interested. I went from manager to manager, and they all promised to get me a deal, but nothing ever materialised. I was devastated. It didn't help that Danny's career was going so well. On the face of it I was happy for him, but deep down I couldn't help feeling both jealous and inferior. Danny was someone, a person in his own right; people looked up to him and respected him. I, on the other hand, was a failure, a washed-up singer with no recording deal.

I wouldn't have minded so much about work had I been a better mother, but I seemed lousy at that as well. It wasn't that the children weren't cared for; they were, but just not by me. I knew that my relentless partying was taking me away from them, and I felt guilty about that, but rather than stop and spend more time at home where I belonged I just carried on. I was an absent mother and I hated myself for that. Danny tried to convince me that I was doing a good job, but I refused to believe it for I knew it wasn't the truth. I may have been a good mother to Daisy when she was young, but that was before the drugs. I remember being at a music festival in Australia in 1997, three months after I had Alfie, and Danny and I being completely out of it on E. I had being talking away to Adam Horovitz, from the Beastie Boys, making no sense whatsoever, gurning like a mad woman, when a girl from Danny's record company came up to me and said, 'Your poor kids!'

'What did you say to me?'

'I said "your poor kids". I really pity your children for having parents like you!'

'Fuck off,' I replied. 'What the hell do you know about us or our kids?'

She looked me up and down, raised her eyebrows and walked off. At the time I may have pretended that I didn't care, but I did. Those words haunt me to this day.

Much as I wanted to give my children the love and the attention they wanted and needed, I just couldn't. My needs always came before theirs. They would come to me in the morning, when I was sleeping off the night before, and try to wake me. 'Not now darling,' I'd say, 'Mummy's having a rest.' They might want to play or talk when I was down, and I would sit there with them but wouldn't interact. If they came into the room and asked me to do something, I would give them the brush-off. 'Darling, I'm on the phone.' 'I've got friends coming round.' 'I'm off out.' 'Watch some T.V and I'll talk to you later.'

My relationship with Danny wasn't much better, in fact things had got so bad between us that earlier that summer we had questioned whether we should carry on. He couldn't cope with my depression and my extreme mood swings, and I resented the time he spent away from me because of his work commitments. We had terrible fights, which usually started after a heavy night out, and would last for days on end. I would get angry with him over the smallest matter and would lash out at him, shouting and screaming at the top of my voice. At one point we took a couple of weeks out from each other, but in the end we both came to the realisation that we couldn't live without each other, that we loved one another, and so we made an effort to make it work, not just for ourselves but for the children as well.

Everywhere I looked in my life there seemed to be chaos, whether it was my relationship with Danny and the children, my career or lack of it, or my dependency on drugs. I no longer seemed to be in control of anything. I thought things couldn't get much worse in those months, but I was wrong, for then came the final nail in the coffin: Danny and I discovered that we were heavily in debt.

It was Danny's manager who broke the news to us in a meeting. 'Do you have any idea how much you spend a month?' he asked us.

We looked at one another and shook our heads. We didn't have a clue.

'Well, last month you spent £20,000.'

'Is that a lot?' Danny asked.

'It's a fuck of a lot, Danny! And what's more you haven't got anything to show for it!' he said. 'If you carry on like this then you'll be bankrupt within a year.'

Danny and I sat there in silence. Neither of us could believe what we were hearing, but then neither of us had kept an eye on our finances. We had just taken it for granted that we were financially secure.

As we went through our finances in that meeting it soon became clear that Danny and I had over-extended ourselves. A year earlier we had moved from our house in Stratford Villas into a beautiful rambling mansion in Willesden, boasting seven bedrooms and a large garden. It had set us back a bit, but we had assumed that we could afford it. Now we were being told that we were going to have to sell it if we wanted to get out of debt. We were devastated, but this was our only option for we seemed to owe money everywhere we looked. I had run up tens of thousands of pounds on my credit and store cards, and they were all at their limit. We owed money to the bank, to the band, to my mother even. In her capacity as an interior designer she had bought furniture and soft furnishings for me and had overseen the decorating work on the house, and I still hadn't paid her back. We had vast overheads. There were school and nursery fees to pay each term, we employed a nanny and a cleaner as well as a PA. Our 'entertaining' bill each month was horrific. There were dinners and lunches at restaurants such as the Ivy and Nobu; there was the wine we bought for our regular parties, the fresh flowers I filled the house with, not to mention the money I was spending on drugs. I didn't think twice about buying three grams of coke if we were going out, which meant that if we had a heavy week of partying ahead of us I was looking at parting with close to a grand just to get out of it. We were living our lives as though we were multi-millionaires, but we weren't.

Danny and I were forced to downsize, and we moved to a house in Rochester Square, Camden. Initially I was heartbroken. Losing the house and so much money just added to my despair. I was depressed that we had ended up in this position, angry and frustrated by our foolishness. Lovely as our new home was, it wasn't Willesden, but over time I learnt to put a brave face and a good spin on it. I told my friends that I was looking forward to moving back to Camden, for I much preferred that part of town, and the more I said this the more I started to believe it myself.

The day of the move came; it was 11 September 2001. The

removal men came early in the morning and I decided to get out of their way whilst they packed the house up. I had just taken some clothes and junk to a charity shop in the early afternoon when my mobile rang.

'Have you heard the news?' said my friend Philippe.

'No – what's happened?'

'A plane has just flown into one of the towers at the World Trade Center and it's on fire.'

'You're kidding me?'

'No, it's on the news.'

By the time I got back to the house the second plane had crashed into the other tower. The removal men had stopped work and were sitting on tea cases in our living-room, watching it on TV in silence. Danny and I joined them.

I am not sure what possessed us, but that night Danny and I took cocaine. We were staying in a hotel in Maida Vale, and two of our friends had come to join us. We sat up all night, glued to the rolling news on TV, high on coke. The following morning, through lack of sleep and the amount of drugs I had taken, I felt so ill I was shaking. Steve had come to our room to collect Alfie to take him swimming with his son at the hotel pool. He looked so fresh-faced and healthy, I felt bad just being in his presence.

'You coming with us?' he asked.

'No, I just can't face it. I'll see you later.'

When I shut the hotel door behind them I felt disgusted with myself. How could I have behaved like that last night? How could I have got off my head when this monumental disaster was unfolding before my eyes? I was a selfish and loathsome person. All my problems I brought upon myself, I had no one else to blame. There were children all over New York who had lost parents in that attack, and here I was, at eleven in the morning, too hung over and sick to take my son for a swim as I had promised.

That morning, on 12 September 2001, I got clean.

19

Twilight

Getting clean this time round was much easier than I thought it would be. As I was coming off cocaine, and not heroin, I didn't have to endure the living nightmare of cold turkey. There were no sweats or shakes, no aches or pains, and I didn't shed a single tear. All I had to do was make the decision to stop using the drug and that was it. It was that simple. I didn't want cocaine in my life any more; I knew that I just couldn't handle it.

I felt the physical benefits of being off the drug almost immediately. I was going to bed at a reasonable hour each night and getting some sleep for the first time in months. When I woke in the morning I wasn't dehydrated or hung over. I regained my appetite and started eating healthily. We had rented a flat in Belsize Park whilst the renovations on our new house in Rochester Square were being completed, and across the street was a gym. I took out a membership, hired a personal trainer and went religiously every other day: exercise became my new addiction. Within just a couple of months I started to get a body I was proud of. I was no longer scrawny from the starving which went with drug abuse, but was lithe and toned. Mentally I felt better too. Taking regular exercise, my trainer had told me when I signed up, would increase my serotonin levels and would help lift my depression, and he was right. After a couple of weeks of my new regime I did feel better about myself. I started to regain my sense of purpose and self-worth.

I made a lot of changes to my life during these months. Now that I was no longer working and was at home all day, I decided that I no longer needed to employ a nanny, which made me happy for I loved being with the children. We still socialised but we stopped being 24-hour party people. We went out to dinner with friends, went to the odd gig and party, but we learnt when to call it a night. If Danny was away then I would stay in with the children. I preferred it that way. At last I seemed to have some structure to my life. I'd wake early in the morning, do the school run and take Frankie to nursery. I'd go to the gym, do the shopping, pick the children up and make them their tea, and by the time Danny came home I would have dinner on the table. It wasn't very rock and roll but I enjoyed it, and I knew that this routine was helping me stay clean. Danny still enjoyed a drink and took drugs from time to time, but I was fine with this. I knew that he didn't have the problems that I had. He could take and leave drink and drugs; he knew when to stop and where to draw the line. With me it wasn't like that – it was all or nothing.

I threw myself into the renovation and decoration of Rochester Square and was determined to make it as beautiful as possible. Because I was clean I wanted the house to be clean as well, and so I painted the entire property white. The walls were white, the floorboards were white; the only colour in the house came from our furniture and paintings, the candy-coloured chandeliers that I hung in every room, and my bathroom, which I painted baby pink. After six months of work the house was finally finished and we were ready to move in.

For some time I had been looking for a piece of fabric to hang over my bathroom window. The house was overlooked at the back by another terrace, and I wanted a piece of material that would give us the privacy we needed but wouldn't block out the daylight. Eventually I stumbled on an old piece of lace, which fitted the window perfectly. It was cream, and I wasn't mad on the colour, so I dyed it fuchsia so that it would be in keeping with the rest of the room. To my surprise and delight it looked amazing. I was showing my new neighbour round the house one day when she commented on the curtain.

'Where did you get that?' she asked enthusiastically.

'Oh, that's something I made. I couldn't find a curtain, so I got some lace and dyed it in the washing machine.'

'I've got to have one! Will you make me one?'

'Are you joking?'

'No, I'm serious! It's beautiful.'

I set to work on her curtain the following day. When she rang a week later to thank me, she asked whether I would be prepared to make a similar curtain for a friend of hers who also wanted one. 'You should start selling them! You'd make a fortune.'

'I couldn't charge people for an old bit of dyed lace.'

'Don't be so stupid! Of course you can. Turn it into a business.'

And so I did. Within just a matter of months I had my own little cottage industry. I sourced the lace from Scotland, dyed it at home and ran it up into curtains, tablecloths and bedspreads.

I was selling only to family and friends at first, but after my house was featured in *Elle Decoration* in a ten-page spread, boutiques around London rang to see whether they could stock my accessories. Before I knew it I had a proper business. The orders were coming in fast and furious and it was a struggle to keep up, but somehow I managed to stay on top of it.

I was surprised by how much I loved my new career. All my life I thought the only thing I wanted to do was sing, but here I was, making lace accessories for the home, and in many ways it was giving me far greater pleasure. I liked working on my own and from home, and I liked having a career that I could combine with family life. I also enjoyed being creative. It was as though I had, quite by accident, found my real vocation in life. Within six months the business had really taken off. I was receiving over twenty orders a week and had started earning proper money again. It was hugely rewarding and liberating.

Coming off drugs was never a problem for me – but staying off them was. I was fine so long as I kept away from temptation, away from people who used regularly, but if I put myself in situations where drugs were around, I admit that I found it difficult. I kept myself to myself when I got clean that year and for six months avoided a lot of my old friends. It wasn't because I had a problem with them, or looked down on them because they used; it was simply because I didn't trust myself in their company. For a time this had been easy. When we had been in the flat in Belsize Park I hadn't had the space or the inclination to entertain – it didn't feel like my home – but when we moved into Rochester Square it was another story. I wanted to show my new house off to my friends. I wanted to fill it with people, and for them to come over to dinner or to hang out during the day when I wasn't working. I was aware that Danny was finding life dull too. He was such a sociable person, and I didn't want to deprive him of seeing people just because of my problems. He had to be able to have his friends, to have a life outside of our relationship, if it was going to survive. They had told me in recovery not to mingle with people who used, but that is, of course, easier said than done, especially when you are in a relationship. Because of the world that we were in, most people we knew took drugs. I couldn't expect Danny to turn his back on all his old music friends because they took the odd line of coke or smoked the occasional joint. I couldn't force him to find a whole new group of clean people to hang out with because that made life easier for me. It just didn't work like that. Life had to go on and I had to learn to be strong. I had to control my addiction, and not have it control me.

Bit by bit I started inviting people over to the house. I knew it was unrealistic of me to put a blanket ban on drugs in the house, so I turned a blind eye to it. If people were using drugs in the sitting-room, for example, I would busy myself in the kitchen. If the coke came out late at night, then I would take myself off to bed. I found ways to deal with it. I made more of an effort to socialise outside the home too. I knew it was important for Danny to do the music scene, and so I began going to more gigs, clubs and industry parties with him. If I thought I couldn't cope, I would simply go home on my own early and watch television or read a book until he came back.

It was around this time that Danny and I made two new friends. Their names were Carl Barat and Pete Doherty and they were in a band called the Libertines. We had watched them play one night at a gig in Notting Hill and had hung out with them afterwards. They were such great guys, so talented and full of spirit, and it didn't take long for us to become close. Danny was forever inviting them round to the house. They would come over for one of my Sunday roasts and still be there two days later. I knew they used, but I found that it didn't bother me in the slightest. If they stayed up all night with Danny, smoking joints or drinking, I would just come down in the morning and start clearing up around them, throwing beer cans away and emptying ashtrays, clucking over them like a mother hen. It used to make Pete laugh. The boys became regular visitors to Rochester Square, and late that summer Carl and his sister Lucie came to live with us for a couple of months. With Carl in residence and Pete forever dropping round, our house soon became party central, but I was happy about that. I proved to myself and to Danny that I could be around drugs and people who used them without being led astray.

It had been a whole year since I got clean, and I truly believed that I was strong enough to carry on along my new path and that I would never take drugs again. In September 2002, however, I relapsed. It happened at a party I was hosting for Supergrass to mark the launch of their latest album. The party was held at a club in Leicester Square and there were over three hundred guests. I had decided that rather than just have the band play their new material I would call upon some of our music friends to perform lounge-style covers of old Supergrass hits. Ed Harcourt, the Libertines, Graham Coxon, Electric Soft Parade and Tricky's muse Martina Topley-Bird all volunteered to take part. I had rather bravely chosen to perform a jazz version of their single 'Alright' and had been rehearsing it for days. I had felt good about the song when I had practised it at home, but on the night itself I was extremely nervous about the performance. It had been eighteen months since I last sang live, and now here I was, about to stand up in front of this massive audience, in front of people like Jay Kay, Jonny Lee Miller and Anita Pallenberg, and sing solo. I was in the ladies' loo, putting on some make-up before I went on stage, when a friend offered me a line of coke. She could see I was nervous and thought that a little pick-me-up would do me good.

'A bit of Dutch courage?' she said, waving the wrap in front of me.

I should have declined, but I didn't. I thought that just a single line might steady my nerves, might get me through it. I only took a small pinch of cocaine, but because I hadn't used the drug for a year it went straight to my head, and by the time I reached the stage I was flying. My hands were sweating and shaking, I couldn't see straight and I was blinded by the stage lights. The music started up and I opened my mouth to sing, but it came out all wrong. I was out of tune and had to speak my way through the lyrics of the first verse. Unable to focus or concentrate, I found myself forgetting the words to the song, even though I had heard it a million times before and it was one of my favourites. All I could remember was the chorus and so I repeated it over and over again. There was a deathly hush in the audience. No one cheered, no one moved, they just stared. Starting to panic, I looked to the wings of the stage, and there was Danny. He was frantically gesturing me to wind the song up.

When I came off the stage I felt so humiliated I wanted to curl up and die, but rather than learn anything from what had just happened to me, rather than admit that I should never take drugs ever again, what did I do? I sought solace in them. I got completely out of my head on them that night and went on a very ugly bender, which lasted three days. And it didn't just stop there either, for within weeks I was back to my old ways, partying round the clock, twenty-four seven.

Although I was always there for the children during the day, I was out nearly every night of the week again, leaving them in the care of a baby-sitter, and on the rare occasions when I did stay in I would invite lots of people round to the house – as well as my dealer.

I stopped going to the gym, stopped eating and sleeping. Overnight my life became completely unmanageable again and I wasn't functioning properly. Orders for curtains would come in, and I would be so out of it, because either I had just taken or I was coming down from drugs, that I would forget all about them. When I did manage to write any of them down I frequently got the measurements or colours wrong. Then the finished products would have to be returned to me and I would have to make them up all over again, which was a waste of both time and money.

I had spent so long getting well, and yet my fall had been so quick. Everything I had built up within the past year, whether it was my work or my relationships with Danny and the children, was unravelling before me, but I did nothing about it. I carried on like this for five months, getting worse and worse, until finally, during one of our daily rows, Danny could take it no more.

'I can't deal with this!' he exploded.

'With what?' I shouted.

'You! I love you, but not like this! I can't cope with you on drugs. It's like living with Jekyll and Hyde. One minute you're clean and the perfect mother, girlfriend, career woman, the next you're bang on the drugs again and behaving like a monster! All you seem to do these days is take drugs. You're chain-smoking fags, you're not sleeping or eating and you're always in a filthy mood. You are screwing up both our lives.'

'If you don't like it, just leave then!' I screamed.

'You know, if you carry on acting like this I just might.'

'Stop lecturing me! You are doing my head in. I'm no worse than you are.'

Deep down I knew that Danny was right. I was behaving like a monster and my life was a mess. If I carried on like this I would have nothing left – no relationship with my kids, no work and no boyfriend – but still I did nothing about it.

Two weeks later I was sitting at my friend Siobhan Fahey's house having tea. Like me, Siobhan had always been interested in anything mystical or spiritual, and that afternoon she had invited a shaman round to the house to give a group of us a talk and a reading. I was sitting on the sofa between a couple of friends when the shaman suddenly singled me out.

'You,' he said, pointing in my direction.

'Me?'

'Yes, you! We know what you are doing,' he said sinisterly. 'You have to follow the white road or your life will not be worth living. You will only find success and happiness if you follow the white road.'

'Yeah, right!' I laughed nervously. I wished that he would leave me alone, for I knew where this was going.

He came over to the sofa, leant over, took my hand and looked me straight in the eyes. 'We know what you are doing. You cannot fool us. All these potions you take, you must stop it, stop it all now, once and for all, or your life will not be worth living. Trust us.'

I was so frightened by what he said that the next day I cleaned up again.

20

A Fond Farewell

It was Gavin who first suggested that Daisy should undergo a paternity test. I remember that Sunday in May 2003 very clearly. Gavin had called the day before and told me that he needed to talk to me about something and asked whether he could come round. Since his marriage to the singer Gwen Stefani in September 2002 Gavin had been spending most of his time in LA. We kept in contact and saw them when they came over to London, but it had been a while since their last trip. As I was in Oxford that evening, I arranged for Gavin to come and see me at Rochester Square the following day.

There had always been a slight question mark over Daisy's true parentage, as there had been a night back in 1988 when, seeking solace after yet another row with Bronner, I went round to Gavin's and we had ended up in bed together. When I realised that I was pregnant I mentioned the night in question in passing to Gavin, but neither of us believed back then that he could really be her father. We had only been together for a single night, as he pointed out, we had been careful, and in any case the dates just didn't add up: Daisy was due on 14 February, Gavin and I had been together in April. It was simple, we concluded at the time: Gavin couldn't be Daisy's father; it had to be Bronner.

When Daisy was a small child she bore what I thought was a striking resemblance to Bronner. She seemed to have both his mouth and his eyes, something his mother was always keen to point out. 'She looks just like him at that age,' she would say as she cooed over her. The fact that Daisy was dark and not fair like Bronner was never an issue for me; I simply thought she had inherited my colouring. But when she hit her early teens, any similarity between the two of them seemed to disappear altogether. Unlike Bronner and me, who were pretty average in height, Daisy was tall. Unlike both of us, she was incredibly long-limbed and had a thick mane of hair.

Just a month or two before Gavin's call I happened to mention this to Danny one night in bed. 'But I thought you said she couldn't be Gavin's because of the dates?' he said to me.

'Yes, but she was born in January, after all.'

'Maybe she was early.'

'Maybe, but she was a pretty healthy size when she was born.'

'So you think she's Gavin's?'

'I don't know . . . I just don't know.'

A fortnight after this conversation I met with a psychic called Mia Dolan, who had come to my house to film a pilot for a television programme. Danny and I had been trying to move from Rochester Square for some time as I was starting to tire of London and wanted to move to the country, but for some reason the house wouldn't sell. So when it was suggested that as part of a TV show I invite a medium into our house and let her discover why it wouldn't shift, I agreed.

'There have been a lot of parties in this place,' Mia said as she moved from room to room. I laughed. How could she have known that? It had been a month since I got clean, and I was determined that I should stay that way after what the shaman had said to me, so I had made a conscious effort in those four weeks to avoid socialising. I had called time on the parties and late-night sessions, and although I wasn't going to meetings or seeing a counsellor I was committed to my path.

'There has been a lot of darkness here too, but this is part of Pearl's old life and she mustn't worry, for it will sell,' Mia continued. Then, turning to me, she said, 'I see you in the country. I have an image of you sitting on a hill with water to the left of you.' I was amazed. I hadn't told Mia that I wanted to move to the country and that I had been looking at properties. All she knew was that I wanted to sell my London home.

Because Mia's reading of the house had been so accurate, at the end of the filming I asked whether she could give me some advice. She agreed and we went into the sitting-room alone. 'Something has been preying on my mind for a while now and I was wondering whether you could help,' I said. 'It's to do with my daughter Daisy. I need to know who her father is. It could be one of two people and I really need to set my mind at rest.' I was embarrassed by this admission, but Mia didn't seem particularly shocked.

'Do you have any photographs of these men? I would need to see a photograph of them before I could tell you.'

I went to the shelf and pulled out some albums. I showed her a photograph of Bronner and then flipped through the book until I found one of Gavin. It wasn't a great picture, for he was standing in a group of people, but it was the only one I had to hand. 'Do you need to see a picture of Daisy?'

'No, this is enough.' She studied the two pictures for a moment and then with an air of confidence placed her finger on Gavin's face and said, 'It's him!'

I was stunned, for I hadn't even identified him in the group. 'Are you sure?'

'Ninety-nine per cent certain. That's what my spirit guides are telling me, and yours. They say look in the eyes, it's in the eyes.'

After Mia left I pulled out all my photographs and sat on the floor poring over pictures of Daisy and Gavin. Mia was right. They did have the same eyes: long and almond-shaped. I then found a picture of Daisy and Gavin together; the resemblance was uncanny.

When I told Danny what had happened that night and showed him the pictures, he laughed at me. 'Look, with all due respect to your beliefs and to this woman, I really don't think you can ring Gavin in LA and suddenly announce that he's the father of your child on the grounds that some mystic said so. He's going to think you've gone mad!'

I knew Danny had a point. Gavin would think I was insane. So it was a huge relief to me when just weeks later he came for that 'talk' at Rochester Square and suggested, off his own bat, that we do a paternity test.

I had arranged for Daisy to be out when Gavin came round that afternoon, with his dog Winston. He explained to Danny and me that this was something that had been at the back of his mind for some time. Because he had just married Gwen and they planned to start a family of their own, he felt it was time to get his house in order. He couldn't have been sweeter about the whole thing.

'If it turns out that she is mine, then I think we need to look at getting her some professional help, some counselling,' he said. 'She is just a child and this could be very disruptive for her.'

'But at least you two get on,' Danny said.

'Of course we do. You know I love her, and that's why I think we need to have the support in place. I don't want her going through any trauma.'

Later that evening Danny, Gavin and I went with our friend Ed Harcourt to watch Radiohead play the Shepherd's Bush Empire. Gavin put a protective arm around me during the gig.

'I'm glad you have agreed to this,' he whispered in my ear. 'And don't worry about anything. It's all going to be fine.'

'I know it will,' I told him, squeezing his hand.

It had been agreed that we wouldn't tell Daisy what was going on until we got the results of the test. As far as she was aware she was going to have a swab taken from her mouth for a routine medical health check. We would only explain what was going on if Gavin turned out to be her father. I was so grateful to Gavin for being so mature and sensitive about the situation, and I told him that I would make all the necessary arrangements. Because he was living in LA and was so rarely in London these days, it made sense for us to do the test as soon as possible as I didn't know when he would be back in town again. Having consulted my GP on the matter and been put in touch with a Harley Street clinic, I rang Gavin the following day to find out when he was free to take the test. There was no answer on his direct line, so I left a message. At first I wasn't concerned that I hadn't heard back from him immediately. I knew how busy he was, but as days passed and the silence grew I knew that something was up. I left message after message but still got no response. I simply didn't understand it.

Days turned into weeks and still no word came from Gavin. It was June and I had gone to Glastonbury with Danny, leaving the children at home in my mother's care. I was getting extremely frustrated by the stalemate with Gavin, not least because in the past few weeks Daisy had been talking about going to America after school to attend college. She told me that she thought she would like to go to a university in Boston so that she could get to know her 'father'. I didn't say anything.

'You don't mind, do you, Mummy?'

'Why did you ask that?'

'Because you never talk about him. You never mention Bronner's name.'

'Why all this sudden interest in your father? Don't you look on Danny as your Dad?'

'Oh, of course I do. I love Danny, but one day I'd like to get to know my real father,' she said.

It was around midnight when my mother called me at Glastonbury, and because of the noise at the festival I didn't hear the phone ring. When I picked up the message early in the morning I was alarmed. 'Pearl, call me as soon as you get this message. It's about Daisy.'

'What is it?' I asked, frantic with worry, when my mother answered the phone. 'Is she OK?'

'Don't worry, she is fine, physically, but I'm not sure about emotionally. Bronner is over here and she's been with him.'

'WHAT! How on earth did that happen?'

'She found him on the net a couple of weeks ago and they've been in contact.'

'Oh God! This wasn't supposed to be like this! How is she?'

'Pretty upset. I think you'd better come straight home.'

Encouraged by a school friend, Daisy had tracked Bronner down via the web. It hadn't been that difficult, since he had just brought out a book and his contact details were on a website. She had e-mailed him, explaining who she was, and to her surprise he had got in touch with her immediately. He said that he would love to meet and catch up with her, and that he would book a ticket and fly to London to see her. Cannily, Daisy suggested that he come over the weekend I was away. But sadly the meeting between Bronner and Daisy had not gone well. I don't think either of them realised how traumatic it was going to be. Through no fault of his own Bronner didn't know how to deal with or act around a fourteen-year-old girl, and Daisy, in turn, was disappointed by the reunion. For so many years Bronner had been a fantasy figure to her, and in her childlike way she had imagined him to be something that he wasn't.

'I don't even look like him,' she sobbed when I got home that afternoon. 'He's small and he's blond and he's got a long nose.'

I didn't know what to say. Fortunately, I hadn't seen Bronner, as he had left for the States by the time I got back to London. Had I run into him, I'm not sure what I would have said or done. I was angry that he had been naïve enough to think that he could just waltz back into Daisy's life like that and that everything would be OK.

To my great relief, after her initial upset Daisy didn't mention Bronner again. It was as though she had banished all thoughts of him from her mind and for a while things, on the face of it, went back to normal. Deep down, however, I was getting increasingly perplexed and bothered about the fact that Gavin still hadn't been in touch. I tried to get in contact with him, but it was to no avail. My calls and messages were ignored, my e-mails went unanswered. I'd always considered Gavin to be one of my best friends in life, and yet now he was giving me the silent treatment and I couldn't understand why. I had only done what he had asked me to do, which was to agree to a paternity test.

In late September I was admitted to the Portland Hospital to have yet another procedure to have cancerous cells removed from my ovaries. I had been reluctant to have the operation that week, because it meant that I was going to miss Zoë's birthday party. I didn't want to let her down, but the pain had got so acute that I didn't have any option.

It was around this time that I sought legal advice about the situation with Gavin. I had gone to see my solicitor with regard to another matter, and at the end of the meeting she asked if there was anything else she could help me with. I had no intention of involving a lawyer in our dispute at this stage; I simply wanted to know what my rights were.

'Do you know anything about family law?' I asked.

'Try me,' she said.

I explained what was going on. 'Do you think I have any legal recourse?' I asked her.

'Yes, you do. The law is pretty straightforward on this matter. If the man in question refuses to take a paternity test, then he will be named as her legal father and as such could be liable for maintenance.'

'Money isn't an issue to me, I just want to know who her father is.'

'Would you like to proceed with this matter? If you do I'd be happy to recommend a solicitor who specialises in this kind of dispute.'

'Thank you, but no. I hope that we can resolve this between ourselves, like adults.'

'It's always the best way,' she said. 'But if you do want help, feel free to call me any time.'

I genuinely hoped and believed that Gavin and I could sort things out between ourselves, both for the sake of our friendship and because of Daisy as well. I didn't want things to get nasty between us; I didn't want to lose him from my life or have to drag him through the courts. He was one of my best friends, after all, and he was Daisy's godfather. I didn't want acrimony, just for things to be sorted. Maybe he had got cold feet, maybe he needed a little time; we would sort it out eventually, I told myself. He would call, we would do the test and, whatever the outcome, we would remain friends. But Gavin didn't call. I waited and waited but no word came.

I had almost given up hope of ever hearing from Gavin again when out of the blue Danny and I received an invitation to a Christmas party that was to be held at his and Gwen's Primrose Hill home. Angry as I was with Gavin, I thought it churlish to say 'no', and I hoped that we might have a minute or two to resolve our situation and finalise a date for the paternity test once and for all. But my hopes were dashed that night at the party. Gavin and I never got a chance to speak.

'Did you find that as awkward as I did?' I asked Danny on the way home.

'Did I ever?' he said. 'I don't really understand why they bothered to invite us.'

I was so down about everything that was going on in my life during that period that over Christmas I resorted to taking drugs again. I suppose I wanted to numb the pain of it all. I didn't want to confront my problems, I didn't want to be sober, I just wanted to get completely out of it. Once again, I stupidly believed that I could use drugs here and there, when I needed that little fix to get me through the day or night, but within just a matter of weeks I was in the grip of full-throttle addiction. I was using every day again, and my mind was all over the place. Danny knew that I was going through a difficult time and thought it best not to confront me over my use. He didn't think I could cope with yet another showdown. From time to time he would gently advise me to lay off the coke and dope, but he stopped short of threatening to leave. He realised that I didn't respond well to shock tactics and, in any case, he didn't want to go; he loved me and was determined to be with me. In the end I didn't use for very long. After six weeks of it I gave up again. But the cycle of stopping and starting was exhausting, for all of us.

It was February 2004 and I had been asked to sing at Ronnie Scott's, the legendary Soho jazz club. After my disastrous performance at the Supergrass launch party I should never have braved the stage again, but when my manager called to say that he had got me a showcase gig there I felt I couldn't refuse, even though I hadn't sung a note for months and had no new material. On the night of the gig I was so high on coke that I could barely stand, let alone sing, but still I took to the stage. Channel 4 had asked whether they might film my set at the club that night and chat to me afterwards, but my performance was so awful, my interview so unintelligible, that the footage inevitably ended up on the cutting-room floor. When the show's producers called to say they'd had to edit me out of the programme, they didn't give the reason why, but then they didn't have to. I knew. I was so humiliated. That's it, I thought, I've really gone and blown it this time. My music career is over.

After that episode I realised I had no option but to give up drugs all over again. My life was already in turmoil, and I didn't need to add to my problems by pouring a whole load of coke on top of them – that would just fuel the fire. On the advice of a friend I started visiting a wonderful drugs counsellor called John McKeown. I realised that if I was going to stay clean this time it wasn't enough just to get my body into shape – I had to work on my mind too. I needed mental support to guide me through my battle with drug addiction, and for the first time since I was with Paul at the Charter Nightingale I finally found someone I could connect with. Like Paul, John didn't judge me, he never looked down on me, he just gave me the time and the space to explore my problems and the experience that made it possible for me to deal with them.

Thanks to being clean and my sessions with John I was beginning to get a sense of perspective back in my life. My business was doing well again, the children seemed to be thriving, and my relationship with Danny was stronger than ever. The only cloud that hung over me was the issue of Daisy's paternity. If only Gavin would agree to the test, then finally I might get some closure in my life, some peace, but another two months had passed and I still hadn't heard from him. It was April, and nearly a year had passed since he had first suggested that he underwent the test. I had really hoped that Gavin and I would sort things out between us, but I now knew that was never going to happen. I had hoped that whatever the test revealed, we would remain friends, but we hadn't spoken to each other since Christmas. I was loath to do it, but I could see now that if I wanted to pursue the paternity issue then I was going to have consult a lawyer. It broke my heart that things had got to this level, but I didn't have any other choice.

One night that month we were sitting round the table having a family supper when I mentioned that I wanted to go on a diet. Since I had got clean I had put on a lot of weight and I hadn't been back to the gym. Danny didn't seem to mind — he hated me being too thin — but I cared.

'Why don't you go on Bronner's diet?' Daisy volunteered.

'What diet is that, then?' I said, trying to sound breezy.

'The blood group diet. It's in that book he gave me — *Eat Right for Your Type* or something.'

'I didn't know he had given you a book.'

'I told you. It's the one he worked as a consultant on. He says certain blood groups can't eat various foods, and if you do you get fat. You're an O, like me, so you should eat lots of meat,' she continued as she watched me carve the roast I had prepared. I smiled.

'Really?'

'Yes, try it.'

I read Bronner's book and followed the diet for a month, but I didn't lose a single pound; if anything I was piling on the weight. I felt lethargic and my skin wasn't great either. I assumed that the diet didn't work and it was just another fad, but when I went to have a blood test during a trip to the doctors I was forced to rethink my position. To my surprise I learnt that I wasn't an O like Daisy; I was an A.

We were sitting in the car a week later driving to Danny's parents' place in Oxford when Daisy asked how my diet was going.

'I've binned it!' I said.

'Why?'

'Because I just put on weight, and in any case I was following the wrong eating plan. My blood group isn't O after all. I'm an A, apparently.'

'Who told you that?'

'My doctor. I'm not sure why I never asked what I was before.'

'But you can't be an A!' she shouted from the back of the car.

'I can be and I am!' I laughed, slightly taken aback by her outburst.

'You can't be because I'm an O! I've done enough biology in school to know that one of my parents has to be an O for me to be one, and Bronner isn't – he of all people should know. So either your doctor is wrong . . . or you're not my mother . . . or he isn't my dad!'

Danny and I looked at each other and then back at her. Tears were streaming down her face. Danny pulled over.

'Oh Daisy,' he said, leaning back and putting his hand on her knee to comfort her. 'We need to have a talk later today.'

She was sobbing uncontrollably. He looked at me, not knowing what to do.

'If Dad isn't my father – who is?' she screamed. I paused. 'WHO IS MY FATHER THEN?'

'It could be Gavin . . .' I whispered.

'GAVIN?'

'Yes, Gavin.'

'But he's my godfather!'

'I know, I know.'

'How long have you known this? Have you been lying to me all my life?' She was, understandably, very angry now. 'Does *he* know? Have you told him?'

'Yes, he does, he is aware of the situation, but it's not certain that he is your father, Daisy. Nothing is set in stone. We need to get to the bottom of it and do a test.'

'When? When can we do the test? I want to know who my father is. I have a right to know. This is about me, *not* you. This is my life! I want you to arrange it soon!'

'I know, darling. I want that too. It's just not quite that simple.'

'Why not?'

'That's a very good question, Daisy. One I wish we could answer,' Danny said with a sigh.

21

Don't Look Back Now

I spoke to Gavin in the summer of 2004 to inform him that I felt I had no choice but to pursue the matter of Daisy's paternity through my lawyers. I didn't want to make the call, but I felt that I now had no alternative. Gavin was not happy. Rather than agree to the test, as I hoped and prayed that he would, he told me that he never wanted to see me again, and with that he hung up. Two weeks later I received a letter from him. He inferred that I was trying to ruin his life and pointedly accused me of messing up my own.

I was angry and deeply hurt by what he was saying. By embarking on this course of action I wasn't trying to destroy anyone's life; that wasn't in my nature. All I wanted to do was discover my child's heritage. I owed it to her, and I owed it to Bronner and to Gavin too – even if it now seemed that he would rather be kept in the dark. I was furious that he chose to suggest that this was all my doing when he was the one who had initiated the whole thing; it had been Gavin who had come to me on the matter and had set the ball in motion, not the other way round as he was now trying to imply. And I couldn't understand anyone thinking that Daisy could be seen as some sort of 'mistake'. She was beautiful, kind and intelligent;

a parent couldn't wish for a better child. Maybe I had messed up my life and made mistakes, but my daughter was not one of them. She was one of my greatest achievements.

I knew that there were people who thought I should leave the matter alone and just get on with my life as it was, but I couldn't. There was no going back, for now that Daisy knew there was a question mark over her parentage she was determined to have it answered, and I had to respect her wish. She wanted to know who her father was once and for all. 'I just need to know who I am,' she said to me one day.

After two months of wrangling between our respective lawyers Gavin finally agreed to the test, though he was far from happy about it. He would take his in LA and we would have ours done in Harley Street. On the day of our appointment Daisy and I went to the clinic together and a nurse sat us down and talked us through the procedure. She would take our DNA by swabbing a small amount of saliva from our mouths. It would be both quick and painless, she said. Our samples would then be sent to a laboratory, where they would be tested alongside Gavin's to see if there was a match. It would be six weeks before we knew the result.

'Are you sure you are happy to go ahead with this, Daisy?' I asked.

'I need to know,' she said simply.

I was driving the car when my lawyer rang to tell me the news. I wasn't that surprised. I suppose I had known for some time what the outcome of the test would be. I called Danny as soon as I put the phone down, and then spoke to my mother.

'Do you want your father and me to be there when you

tell Daisy?' she asked. 'She might be very upset, and she could do with as much love and support as she can get.'

'I don't think she is going to be upset, Mum,' I said. 'On the contrary, I think she is going to be over the moon.'

Although she hadn't said as much, I knew that deep in her heart Daisy was longing for Gavin to be her father.

'Are you sure?' she beamed when I told her the result.

'Certain,' I said.

'Have you spoken to him yet?'

'Not yet, no. I wanted to talk to you first.'

It was, of course, quite understandable that Daisy should want Gavin to be her father. Because he left us when she was so young, she didn't have a bond with Bronner, but with Gavin there had always been a connection. He had come to her sports days when she was a child, attended her parent/teacher meetings and watched her in the school play. He came to her birthday parties when he was in town, and if he was away there was always a card and a present waiting for her. There was no denying it, Gavin had played a major role in her life.

Later that day I e-mailed Gavin to find out how he wanted to handle the situation from here on. Was he planning to call Daisy and talk to her? Or did he want to wait until he was back in London and see her face to face? Now that we had the result, I thought he would get straight back to me as he would want to sort things out, but there was no response. Once again, I'd hit a wall.

When Daisy realised that I had been unable to get hold of him that evening she took matters into her own hands and called him herself. Eventually she succeeded in speaking to him but their conversation did not help matters, and in many respects, made it worse. He appeared more concerned with venting his anger about my behaviour than engaging with his daughter.

By pursuing the matter of Daisy's paternity I hadn't meant to do anything other than to discover the truth. I didn't want money from Gavin, and I didn't expect him to suddenly be the perfect father either. I did hope that in time the two of them would form a relationship beyond what they had already, but I wasn't expecting anything more than that. Daisy already had a father in Danny. Biologically he may not have been her dad, but in every other respect he was. From the outset he had raised her and loved her as if she were his own.

All this was very hard on Daisy. She was confused and hurt, and spent most days in tears. I felt helpless, I simply didn't know what to do. I spoke to my counsellor John and asked his advice. He said that he would be more than happy to talk to her, and also that if she would rather see someone else he could recommend another therapist.

Daisy wasn't having any of it. 'I don't need a psychiatrist to tell me why I'm feeling like this!' she said. 'Of course I'm upset. Wouldn't you be?' I couldn't argue with that. Fortunately for Daisy she had a strong network of support to help her through this period. Both Danny's and my parents gave her a lot of time and love during those months; her teachers and school friends were aware of what had happened and rallied round her, and Zoë was her shoulder to cry on when she felt that she couldn't talk to me.

It is a testimony to my daughter's maturity and strength of character that as time went on she was able to cope with the situation, and after she got over her initial hurt she dusted herself down and got on with her life. She persevered with Gavin, determined to forge some kind of relationship with him. When he was in LA she would e-mail him with her news, and if she heard on the grapevine that he was in London, she would call him and try to meet up with him. And things did get better. From time to time, he would ask her round to his house.

Painful though this whole episode was, it did have its flipside, for it brought Daisy and me closer together. I couldn't have loved my child more than I did already, but now that I was no longer hiding something from her I felt a barrier had come down. We spent a lot of time together talking things through, making sense of it all, and I was astounded by her level-headedness. Unlike me at that age, Daisy had a wise head on those tiny little shoulders. I wrote to Bronner to explain what had happened. I told him that I had never intended to fool him and that in all honesty I had, until the year before, always believed that he was her father. I wasn't surprised by his response. He was angry, quite understandably, but he acknowledged that he was also aware of the fact that since the day he had left us I had never asked him for anything, and had supported Daisy myself.

I cannot pretend that any of this was easy for me. I was upset for Daisy, and even though I knew I had ultimately done the right thing by her, I couldn't help wondering whether I had handled it properly. I was suffering from guilt about Bronner, and my feelings toward Gavin oscillated between anger and remorse. I was still upset by everything that had happened and I couldn't help feeling sad about the friendship we had lost.

It had never been my intention to ask Gavin for maintenance

for Daisy, and I had told my solicitor this when we spoke in the weeks after the result came through. She was taken aback. 'Are you sure?' she asked.

'Money was never my motivation in this – you know that. I just needed to know whether he was the father or not. I don't want his money.'

'*You* may not want his money, but what about Daisy? Who maintains her now? Who pays her school fees, for example? Who puts the food on the table? Pays for her clothes?'

'We do, well, Danny does really,' I admitted. 'But he's happy with that, he always has been, it's just the way he is.'

'But that was before you knew.'

'Danny doesn't want money either, he isn't that kind of person.'

'Look, Pearl, maybe Danny has been happy to support Daisy all these years, but is it really fair to expect him to carry on doing so now? He's taken care of her for nearly ten years. As your lawyer I could advise you to seek back maintenance, but if you're not prepared to do that, at least consider getting Gavin to help you with her future.'

After what had happened with the paternity test I was loath to contact Gavin again, but I could see that my solicitor had a point. Even though it would never have been an issue to him it wasn't fair for Danny to have to carry on supporting Daisy. If I'd had the money I would have taken care of her myself but, successful though the lace company was, I wasn't earning enough to cover her maintenance on my own.

'Maybe I should take her out of private school,' I suggested to Danny that evening.

'Why on earth would you do that?'

'Because it's not fair on you . . .'

'I don't care what's fair on me. I will always support her – you know that. What I care about is what's fair on her. Take her out of school and you take her out of the place where she is happy and secure, where her friends are. I think she has been through enough upheaval this year already, don't you? And what about her brothers? Do you think it's fair that they should be entitled to a private education and she shouldn't, just because of biology? It isn't right.'

I could see where Danny was coming from, but even though he promised that night to carry on supporting Daisy, I wasn't comfortable about it. I called my solicitor the next morning, and negotiations over Daisy's future maintenance began. In the end it would take us over a year, and a day in court, to agree on a reasonable settlement.

It is at times like this when you look to your friends for support. As I quickly discovered, however, apart from a handful of people who were always there for me, I didn't really have any true friends. I had a wide social circle, of course, but few of them really cared about what was going on; they either didn't want to get involved or simply weren't interested.

'Oh come on, cheer up,' they would say. 'It's not the end of the world! What you need is a big night out and then you'll be OK. No point staying in feeling sorry for yourself.'

I had been staying in a lot during those months. Being clean, I had no desire to go out, and because of what was going on with Daisy I wanted to spend as much time at home with her as I could. Before I knew it, summer had come and gone and it was November, and Danny and I had just received an invitation to a bonfire party in the country. 'I think we should go,' said Danny. 'It would be good to get out of London for the weekend, out of the house even, and they said bring the kids . . . You never know, we might even have fun!'

I knew Daisy wouldn't be coming as she had a party of her own to go to that night, so I accepted the invitation on behalf of Danny, me and the boys. As it was out of London Danny suggested that we make a weekend out of it, so we planned to stay the night in the country and the following day take the kids on an outing. After everything that had happened that summer I was looking forward to getting out of London, but to be honest I was dreading the party. Stupid as it might sound, I have had a lifelong fear of fireworks, and I knew that whilst everyone was having a merry old time around the bonfire I would be cowering in the house until the bangs had stopped. But there was another reason why I didn't have a good time that night: there were just far too many drugs around. A lot of people there seemed to be high that night, and I knew that in the state of mind I was in I just couldn't be around them. I had been seeing a lot of John in those weeks and, knowing how vulnerable I was feeling, he told me to avoid any situation where drugs were involved, for he knew I could be tempted. 'It isn't the answer,' he said. 'You know that from your past history.'

I took heed and drew strength from his words, and for a time it worked and I managed to resist, but as the evening went on and people got progressively out of their heads, I started to feel increasingly uncomfortable. Not knowing what to do I went and sat in the car and rang Zoë. It was around 9.30, the fireworks had stopped, the music was thumping and the wine and drugs were flowing. 'I can't deal with this any more. What should I do?'

'Pearl, just leave, you don't have to be there.'

'But what about Danny and the kids?'

'What about them? The kids have had their party, seen the fireworks, done the bonfire, and as for Danny, just say you want to leave – he'll understand. Just go. Get out of there before you do something that you really regret!'

I got out of the car, rounded up the boys, who were playing outside, and eventually found Danny, who was in the house. He was completely drunk.

'Danny, I think we should go home . . .'

'Why?'

'Because . . . because I just can't cope with this,' I whispered.

'But I don't want to go!' he said loudly.

'Why are you making him go? You're always getting him to leave; you're such a killjoy these days, Pearl,' jeered a rather well-oiled girl.

'Oh, you're not dragging him home again, are you?' sneered another guest.

'I am actually, darling,' I said to them. 'You know what? It's late, I'm not feeling that great and my children need to go to bed, so if it's OK with you I think we might leave and go back to our hotel now.'

Somehow I managed to get Danny into the car. 'I was having a really good time!' he said sulkily.

'Well, good for you! I wasn't! If you want to stay, then just stay. I don't want to fight about this, I haven't got the energy,' I said, gesturing to the passenger door. 'I'll pick you up in the morning if you want to stay up, but I'm going back to the hotel.'

By the time we got back to our B&B Danny's mood had

lifted. We were lying on the bed together and Danny, still a little merry from all the beer and wine he had consumed, flicked on the television. It was the Jonathan Ross show. 'Oh, good,' he said. 'I like this programme.'

'. . . And now . . .' boomed Jonathan from the television set, 'please give a warm welcome to my next guest . . . the very lovely . . . Gwen Stefani!'

Great! That's bloody all I need right now, I thought, trying to grapple Danny for the remote so I could switch channels. Danny thought this was hysterical. 'Come on, babe, try and see the funny side. You come the whole way to the country to go to a party to take your mind off things, and there's Gwen on the TV! You've got to admit it's quite amusing.'

The following morning we were woken early when Alfie and Frankie came bounding on to our bed. 'Let's go!' they screamed in unison. 'Let's go to the fish farm!'

'God, I'm glad you made me come back last night!' Danny groaned, as Alfie pulled at the duvet. 'I'm not feeling so great as it is.'

'When are we going to the fish farm?' Frankie yelled.

'Soon!' Danny shouted back from beneath his pillow. 'But not until you have both brushed your teeth and I've got my head together!'

We had a wonderful family day out at a local trout farm, and as I watched Danny deal with the boys and his hangover I started to feel better about things. So my life wasn't perfect, I had my problems, but at least I had my family. That moment my phone rang. It was a friend who had been at the party.

'You were right to escape when you did,' she said. 'I didn't go to bed until seven this morning.'

'You don't sound very good . . .'

'I'm not. In fact I feel terrible.' She started to cry.

'Are you OK, darling?' I asked.

'No, not really . . . I'm so unhappy . . . so, so unhappy.' She was sobbing so hard now, I found it difficult to hear what she was saying.

'What is it? What's wrong?'

'Everything is wrong. I hate my life, I hate myself . . . Pearl, I really think I need to get clean. I think I need to go to rehab.'

'Are you serious?'

'Yes, I just can't live this life any more . . . I want to get it together, like you have.'

'OK, look, don't worry. I'm still in the country at the moment, but as soon as I get home I'll call you.'

I hung up the phone. 'What was all that about?' asked Danny.

'You don't want to know. I'll tell you what, though, I am *so* glad that I don't take drugs any more.'

22

It's Over

'How did you feel about leaving the party early?' John asked during my weekly counselling session, a couple of days after Bonfire Night.

'I knew it was the right thing to do.'

'Why was that?'

'Because I knew I just didn't want to be there. It wasn't the right place for me to be. It was too dark. It made me realise that I just can't live that life any more. I've made a conscious decision not to take drugs and I have to stick to that. I felt strong for walking away that night, but I'm not going to sit here and pretend it was easy. I didn't want to walk away from friends.'

As an experienced drugs counsellor John knew how difficult staying clean was and understood that every day was a struggle. Having examined my past history, my yo-yo periods of clean time and my subsequent relapses, he advised me that if I was going to keep on my path then I would have to make some serious changes to my lifestyle. It wasn't enough just to decide to get clean; I had to remain that way, and if that was going to happen I would have to keep myself clear of temptation. 'Change your playmates, change the playground,' he would say. 'That's easier said than done,' was my reply. 'These people are my friends and I can't keep hiding from them. So some of them take drugs, I just have to accept that and learn to deal with that. I can't hold them responsible for my addiction, that's down to me.'

'You're absolutely right but, on the other hand, can you not see that by hanging out with people that use you are continually allowing yourself to be put in a compromising situation – one that you might not be ready for?'

I knew that John was right. Much as I loved my friends, I was finding it increasingly difficult to socialise with the ones who used. I didn't want to be seen as the party pooper, the killjoy who was constantly dragging her boyfriend home just when things were warming up. I didn't like having to take myself up to bed at night just because people were partying. I would hear the raucous laughter and the revelries kicking off below stairs and wonder what was going on. I'd feel sad that I could no longer be part of it all, that I was disjointed from the group, and with those thoughts I would have to switch on the television and put the volume up high to drown out the noise in order to find some sense of peace. I hated going to bed at ten at night but, without narcotics, that's when my body started shutting down. I was a young woman, but I felt like an old lady.

Of course, I knew that it was possible to have a social life without drink or drugs; it's just that a lot of my friends, at that time, didn't share that view. There were no evening trips to the cinema or the theatre, no quiet, home-cooked dinners or lazy Sunday brunches. In the world I moved in it was all about deriving as much fun and pleasure as you could from life, and to do that it was almost a prerequisite to be off your head. I remember one evening, for example, inviting a friend over for a girly supper and a chat on a Sunday night whilst Danny was away. Because I knew she liked a glass of wine I had made sure I had a bottle in the fridge for her, and I had no problem with that, but I was slightly taken aback when she pulled out a gram of coke from her handbag as I prepared the salad, and started racking up lines on the kitchen table in front of me.

'Here, I'm cutting you a nice, big, fat one,' she said, as she spliced the white powder with her credit card.

'Darling, you know I can't do that, I'm clean.'

'Oh come on, babe! Don't be so boring. We'll just have a couple and I promise not to tell anyone – not even Danny.'

'I think I'll pass on it, I'm not really in the mood tonight.' I tried to sound as breezy as I possibly could, but I was both angered and hurt that she could be so insensitive.

'OK, suit yourself,' she said with a shrug before hoofing up both lines. Needless to say, she didn't touch a morsel of the food I had prepared for her that evening.

It wasn't easy staying away from the 'playground'. There were times when I felt isolated and very alone. I missed being part of a gang and seeing my friends, and I was growing increasingly tired of my hermit-like existence, but I knew that if I was going to stay clean I just had to keep myself to myself.

'Can't you just go out and have a good time without doing coke?' a friend asked.

'Not at the moment,' I said. 'It's different for you; you can do drugs at your whim and keep it under control, but I can't. I know that now. It's just not in my nature. I can't do the odd line like you can, I have to take the whole gram. I'm an addict. It's all or nothing with me.'

December came and I steered clear of the festivities. 'I'm simply not up for partying this year,' I told Danny as we made plans for Christmas. 'I just want to spend the holiday with the kids. This time of year is all about them, after all, isn't it?' To my great relief Danny agreed and we spent Christmas together alone with the children and had a wonderful time. I knew that so long as I stayed away from situations where drugs were around I was fine, but unless I locked myself away at home for ever and threw away the key I could never guarantee that was going to happen. I knew that what people did in their own lives, in their own time, in their own homes, was up to them, not me. I may have been clean, but I was not going to start being puritanical; my issues with drugs were my own and I had to learn to deal with that.

With all the knowledge I had, it probably wasn't the best idea to agree to go to a large house party in the country, but in late December that's exactly what I did.

John had his reservations about the trip and voiced them from the start.

'Are you sure you are up to it?' he asked.

'I think so. It's not like I'm going to some massive party,' I lied. 'It's just a weekend away in a rented cottage.'

'What if people are using around you?'

'That's just something I will have to deal with. I'll go to bed.'

'Are there any clean people going?'

'Not all my friends take drugs, you know!'

'Well, just stick with people you feel safe around. Staying clean is all about self-protection.'

It didn't take long for the drugs to come out on that first night. My friends did their best to shield me from the fact that some members of the party were using, but as the evening progressed it became increasingly obvious to me what was going on. I had taken enough drugs in my life to know when someone was on them. I was touched that they tried to keep it away from me, but when people kept peeling off from the party to slip into the loo or a bedroom and returned minutes later wide-eyed and chatty, I knew what they were up to.

'Are you OK with this all?' Danny asked when we were alone in our bedroom.

'I'm fine, I really am. They are just having fun, that's all. What am I supposed to do? I just have to ignore it and get through tonight.'

I spent the next hour of the evening in my bedroom. I knew that I would eventually have to rejoin the group, and I was slightly dreading it, but I didn't have much choice. It was too early for me to call it a night; I had to go back to the party. I went downstairs and looked for Danny but couldn't find him. I tried the sitting-room.

'Is Danny in here?' I asked as I put my head round the door.

'No, but come on in. Where have you been all night?'

I didn't want to look anti-social, so I came in and took a place on the sofa. At the far end of the room a group of people were sitting round a table taking coke. I caught myself staring at them.

'Do you want a line?' asked one of them.

'No, no, that's cool, I'm fine,' I said.

I tried to join in the conversation but it was difficult for me. Everyone was so animated, so full of energy and life, and I just sat there feeling flat and strange, not knowing what to say. I strolled over to join my friends at the end of the room.

'You're sure you don't want one, Pearl?' the man asked again, pointing at the mound of coke on the table.

I stalled. I knew I shouldn't.

Everyone was looking at me, waiting for an answer.

I wanted to resist, and I knew I should, but I didn't. I just couldn't help myself.

'OK, but just a tiny one . . .' I said.

Someone cut me a line, whilst another rolled me a banknote. I hovered over it, I knew exactly what I was doing, but I still didn't stop. I took that note and snorted that line and I would be lying if I said that I didn't enjoy it. And yet, although I take complete responsibility for my actions, what surprises me, when I look back on that night now, is that despite knowing that I was clean not one person in that room intervened. No one tried to stop me from taking that line of coke. No one said: 'Pearl, what the hell do you think you are you doing?' All they did when I finished my line was cheer.

'She's back!' shouted one of the group. 'Pearl is finally back!'

Danny wasn't surprised by the fact I used that night. He suspected that I might fall off the wagon earlier that evening. Not everyone at the party was taking cocaine, but there was a lot of spliff being smoked, a lot of alcohol being drunk, so it wasn't the best environment for me to be in. 'Just take it easy with the coke,' he whispered to me when he joined me in the sitting-room.

'I'm only going to do a bit, then I'll stop,' I said. Famous last words – I must have taken at least twenty lines that night, far more than anyone else in the room, and by the time I made my way up the stairs in the early hours of the morning I was completely out if it. Seeing the state I was in, one friend finally did take me aside. 'Please don't do this to yourself, Pearl. You've done so well being clean. I've been so proud of you, and this just doesn't suit you.'

I should have taken on board what she said, but I didn't. I used all weekend, and when we returned to London I carried on. Danny was dismayed. He thought once I got home I would stop and get clean again, but I refused. I even cancelled all my meetings with John. One single line of cocaine had sent me on a downward spiral, and I was now using more than I had ever done. I was buying coke and was using it morning, noon and night; I smoked joints, crack and opium; and on one occasion during those weeks I even took heroin.

'Why are you doing this to yourself?' Danny asked.

I didn't have an answer.

'You have got to stop this, you've got to get clean again. Please, Pearl, I just can't sit back and watch you destroy your life.'

I wouldn't listen to him. I just felt that I couldn't stop, that I was on a rollercoaster I couldn't get off. The drugs did nothing for me, of course. I'd get high but I never felt happy. I was listless and depressed and I couldn't stop crying. I hated my life, and I hated myself.

I truly believed that things couldn't get much worse for me during those weeks, but I was wrong. At the beginning of February an article appeared in the press that would send my world crashing down on me. According to the story, which was splashed across the front page of a red-top Sunday news-paper, Danny and I had been involved in what they described as 'wife swapping sessions' with two well-known actors during a summer holiday in 2001.

I didn't read the story that morning; I simply couldn't face it. In any case, even if I had wanted to see the paper it would have been impossible for me to get to a newsagent. Herds of photographers had gathered round the house, waiting to catch a glimpse of us, and they stayed camped out there for days. It was a strange position to find ourselves in. Whilst we may have been known within the music industry, our celebrity had never gone further than that. Now, overnight, Danny and I had become tabloid fodder, known to hundreds and thousands of people – not for our music, or for anything we had done creatively, but for our private lives. It was mortifying.

I spent the next few days in tears, unable to move from my bed. My family couldn't have been more supportive to me, but their kind words did nothing to alleviate my anguish. I knew that all the coverage of our lives had brought shame upon them. I was deeply concerned about the impact this would have on the children. I feared that they would be teased and bullied at school, that someone might say something to them. It turned out that I had nothing to worry about, for their teachers and friends rallied round them. Zoë tried her best to comfort me. 'It really isn't the end of the world, and it will all die down in a couple of days,' she said. But the story didn't die down. Over the next week it just grew and grew like some kind of monster with a life of its own.

I carried on using through this period. I knew that it wasn't sensible, but it was the only way that I could get through it all. I needed to feel numb. I wanted to get out of it. I just couldn't face what was going on as a sober person.

Two weeks after the story broke we went to the Caribbean. I had been commissioned by *Elle* magazine to write a travel piece, and so Danny and the children and I flew to Grenada.

One of our closest friends, the actor Rhys Ifans, came with us. I was grateful to be getting out of town but even though we were heading to paradise I couldn't help but feel, as the plane touched down on the island, that I had left my soul behind in London, burning in some inferno of my own creation. Here I was in the Caribbean, thousands of miles away from home, but still I couldn't get that city out of my head. If I could just get out of there once and for all, maybe then I could finally extricate myself from the chaos and madness that was my life there, but I just didn't know how I was going to do it. For years I had dreamt of moving to the country. I had been actively looking for houses, and had even found a couple that I liked, but in order to move we had to sell our house in London first, and for some reason it just wouldn't budge. I was beginning to think that it must be cursed, for every time we came close to a deal it would fall through at the last moment. At the beginning of the year we thought we might have a buyer. A couple were interested in Rochester Square, but they were also having problems selling their own house, so I didn't hold out much hope.

We had only been at the hotel in Grenada for a couple of hours when my mobile rang. I was tempted not to answer it – I had come here to escape all that, after all – but something or someone was telling me to pick up the call, and I was glad that I did for it was my estate agent. 'I've got good news for you, Miss Lowe,' he said. 'You won't believe this but Rochester Square has finally sold. The couple exchanged this morning, so you'd better start looking for somewhere else to live!'

I didn't waste any time. I began my search for a new house there and then. As Danny and Rhys headed to the beach with the kids, I went on the hotel's computer and found a house to rent on the internet within less than an hour.

When I showed Danny the details later that day he couldn't believe it. 'Where is it?' he asked.

'Hampshire.'

'It's incredible! It's everything we ever dreamt of.'

'I know. I couldn't believe it myself.'

'What are we going do? We're here for another two weeks.'

'Don't worry, I've already called the estate agents. I've made an appointment to see it the day that we get back.'

'You move quickly . . .'

'I wasn't going to take any chances. I have a very strong feeling about this house, Danny. I really think that we are meant to be there.'

Although happy to have finally sold Rochester Square and to be moving from London, I was still suffering inside. The events of the last few months had really got to me, and I found it difficult to relax and enjoy myself on that holiday. I felt bad that I had relapsed, was haunted by the tabloid story and, even though I was surrounded by the people I loved, I felt desperately alone. Danny and Rhys did their best to raise my spirits.

'It's just a story, yesterday's news,' Danny would tell me when I got low. 'So some people think you're a bit rock and roll – who cares? They don't know you, they don't see the real person; all they see and believe is what they want to, and you just have to accept that. Worse things in life happen. Look at you, look at what you've got. You've got me and three beautiful, healthy children, that's what matters. Most people would kill for what you have.'

I heard what he was saying but I still found it hard to pull myself out of my depression. As I sat on the white sandy beach that afternoon, watching Danny play with the kids in the turquoise sea, I tried to feel positive but it was a struggle.

One afternoon while we there I went to a yoga class, hoping that a session might alleviate some of my tension. My teacher was a guru, and although I tried to put on a brave face, he picked up on my anxiety and distress during that first session. After the class he pulled me back.

'If you don't mind me saying, you seem deeply troubled. You aren't happy in your life, are you?'

'Not really, no,' I admitted.

'Would you like to talk about it?'

Maybe it was because he was a stranger, maybe I just needed someone to talk to, but at once I felt completely at ease with this man, and during that first conversation together I was totally up front with him about all that was going on.

'It is possible to change your life round, you know,' he said to me as we sat on the beach, staring out to sea.

'How?'

'You just need to live a different life, follow another path.'

'But I keep doing that and it just doesn't seem to work.'

'It's not working because you won't allow it to. You follow the path but you aren't really sure why. You need to get in touch with your spiritual side, and then you will get to the root of your problems and you will have the strength to carry on your journey.'

'You really think that will work?'

'Yes, because I believe that you are a very spiritual person.'

'You do?'

'Yes, but you just can't see it yet. You can't see it because you have blurred your vision with all these drugs that you have taken. When you put those down you will be able to see clearly. See life as it really is. You need to step out of the darkness and into the light.'

23

Feral Betty

The day after we got back from Grenada we went to see the house in Hampshire, and before I even stepped through the front door I knew that I had to live there. There was something so enchanting about the place, so tranquil. The house itself dated back to the fourteenth century and was set in seven acres of land. To the right of the property, at the foot of a bank, was a river, with a bridge that led over to woodland; at the back was a large rambling garden. It was so quiet and peaceful there, the only noise to be heard other than the birdsong was the babbling sound of water. It was just as the psychic Mia Dolan had described when she gave me that first reading: a house in the country with water to the side of it.

'This is it, this is where I want to live,' I told Danny.

'You haven't even seen inside yet.'

'I don't have to. I know this is the right place for us. I can feel it.

'What if it's not big enough?'

'Then we'll sleep in tents!'

As I walked through the house I instinctively knew that I would be happy there. I could see myself cooking supper at the Aga, Danny playing football with the boys in the garden, teaching them to fish on the banks of the river. Daisy could invite her friends over for weekends, and we'd have lunch out on the terrace when the weather was good. We'd spend our evenings by the fire or watching movies in the sitting-room; we'd go for long walks, take the kids to the beach, and we'd get a dog.

'What do you think?' asked the estate agent when Danny and I had completed our tour.

'It's absolutely perfect,' he said.

Driving back home through the London traffic I knew that we had made the right decision. The novelty of city life had worn off many years ago; neither of us wanted to be there any more, and it was time to go. The boys had reached an age where they were getting bored with London life. I didn't want them growing up in front of the television set. I wanted them to have the freedom to run around, to explore the great outdoors. I knew that Daisy wasn't mad on the idea of moving to the country. Like most teenage girls, all she ever seemed to want to do those days was meet her friends and go on shopping trips or to the movies, but the house was only an hour away from London by train and she could always have her friends to stay – we had room for that now. It would be a fresh start for all of us, a new chapter in our lives.

After my conversation with the guru I knew that I had to get clean again, and so, on 6 March 2005, one week after we returned from Grenada, I put down the drugs once and for all. I tackled my recovery very simply. I didn't enrol in another in-patient rehabilitation programme. I didn't head off to some fancy boot camp in Arizona either. I just stopped using. I started seeing John again on a weekly basis and regularly attended NA meetings. I found myself a lovely sponsor and started writing down my steps, which I would read to her when we met up. I was on a mission, and nothing was going to take me off my path this time.

A month after I got clean, Danny and I went away for the night to a country house hotel to celebrate my birthday. I wasn't in the mood for a big party that year. All I wanted was to spend the evening alone with him, and I have to say that it was one of the nicest birthdays I have ever had. After a delicious dinner we went back to our room and watched television in bed. There was a documentary about foetal development, and we were both glued to it. 'I wish I'd known all this when I was pregnant,' I said to Danny.

'Why?'

'Because if I had known what damage you could do to an unborn child I would have lived a much healthier life.'

I hadn't been feeling very well for the last couple of weeks, as it happened. I'd been tired and generally felt under the weather. At first I thought I must have picked up a bug, but when the symptoms persisted I concluded that it was probably down to getting clean: all those toxins I had taken were finally being expelled from my body. Having had three children I suppose I should have seen the signs, but it was in fact Daisy who first suspected I was pregnant a week later.

'I can't be!' I said when she suggested it to me.

'You won't know unless you do a test.'

'Oh don't be silly, Daisy, I'm not pregnant.'

Daisy was having none of it. She not only marched me round to the chemist, but she stood outside the bathroom door while I took the test.

Daisy was right, I was pregnant. It was amazing. In the last couple of years Danny and I had talked about having another baby, but it just hadn't happened and we had almost given up hope, so neither of us could really believe it when the test result turned out to be positive. We were overjoyed. When we later discovered that I was having a baby girl, it was the icing on the cake. Frankly, I wouldn't have minded what sex the baby was, but Danny wanted another daughter, and Daisy and the boys were desperate for a sister. We decided that we would name her Betty after my paternal grandmother, whom I adored.

From the moment I discovered that I was pregnant with Betty I believed that she was a gift from God, my miracle baby, and it felt like affirmation of this when I realised that she had been conceived on 7 March, the day after I stopped using. As far as I was concerned Betty was always destined for this world, but she wouldn't come to me until I was clean.

After so much darkness in our lives, Danny and I seemed finally to be heading towards the light. There was a lot to look forward to that spring. We were thrilled about the baby, we were excited about the move to the country, and we were about to take the children on a month-long holiday to Deia, in Majorca, before taking possession of the house in August. It was like a new beginning and I felt genuinely happy about life. Because so many positive things were happening to me at that moment I didn't miss the drugs at all. In fact now that I was pregnant I found the very idea of drugs abhorrent; I kept thinking back to the documentary I had watched about foetal development and would feel quite sick if someone so much as mentioned them.

As soon as we returned from Deia we moved into our new house. Initially I was in good spirits; the sun was out, everyone was happy and I was having fun putting my mark on our new home. When September came, however, I suddenly hit a low point and began to feel very negative and down about everything again.

My problems started when Daisy announced towards the end of the summer that she didn't want to leave London. She had become very attached to a boyfriend, and he was trying to persuade her to stay in town. I was at my wits' end, not least because Daisy had just got into a top private school in Hampshire and I couldn't believe that she was about to throw away this opportunity, all for the sake of a teenage fling. We talked it through, over and over again, and I tried to reason with her, but she refused to change her mind. She told me in no uncertain terms that she wasn't prepared to leave her boyfriend behind and she didn't want to move schools either. In the end I realised that I couldn't force her to come, and so it was decided that she would stay with my parents in London during the week and come and see us at weekends. I was unhappy about the arrangement. Although I knew my parents would take good care of her, I really felt that at sixteen she was too young to fly the nest.

I had always hoped that moving to the country would bring us closer together as a family, but now that Daisy was staying in London the exact opposite seemed to be happening. I felt terribly lost without her. It didn't help that Danny had gone on tour with the band to Japan that month, or that the boys had started school. After I dropped them off in the morning I found myself all alone, with nothing to do, no one to talk to.

I felt very isolated, and the more time I spent on my own, the more time I had to think, which just compounded my sense of misery. I became quite melancholic during those weeks.

I knew that I had a lot to be grateful for. I had been given another chance at life, even though I probably didn't deserve it. I was glad that I had stopped taking drugs and felt better for that both mentally and physically. I had my house, my new life in the country, my relationship with Danny had improved and we were really getting on well together. Daisy may have wanted to stay in London, but I knew that the move was good for the boys. It hadn't taken them long to adapt to their new way of life, and they had both settled into school and had quickly made new friends. On the outside my life couldn't have been much better than it was at that moment, but inside I was suffering.

I tried to be positive about things, and put my best foot forward, but I found it hard, for I was haunted by memories of my past. Now that I was clean and sober I could think clearly about all that had happened, about how I used to be, and that was at times very painful for me. When I looked back at how I was on drugs I was filled with remorse and guilt. I had always loved my children more than life itself, but there was no denying that at times I hadn't been the best of mothers. When I was using I always put my needs and desires before theirs, which was selfish and wrong of me. To my eternal shame I had let people and parties take me away from my family, and I would always regret the time I lost with them. I remembered the occasions when I had emotionally pushed them away because I was too tired or too hung over to deal with them. I remembered the countless children's parties I had forgotten to take them to because I was just too out of it to keep a mental note of anything. I remembered the time when I took Alfie on an outing to the zoo for a classmate's birthday and when I arrived, another mother, who was a friend of mine, was so appalled by the sight of me that she offered to take over.

'God, Pearl, you look so tired. You look green – and you're shaking. Did you go to bed last night?'

'Yes, but only for a couple of hours,' I admitted.

'Go home and get some sleep! I'll watch Alfie for you and see you later.'

My friend was right. I was tired because I had stayed up partying until the early hours the night before, and I felt terrible, so I took her up on her offer.

My children were never neglected, but that wasn't the point. The fact was, I should have given them far more than I did. I was always there for them and tried to do my best by them, but I wasn't giving them one hundred per cent of my attention and I felt perennially guilty about that.

Thanks to my addiction I'd missed out on so much during those years, and that upset me too. I had screwed up my music career because of my drug-taking, and wasted so many opportunities that had come my way. I couldn't help feeling a sense of regret about it all, and I found myself wondering what I might have become had I not used. Because I was always either high or coming down I could never really fully appreciate anything that came my way. There was the occasion when I visited Venice for the first time and spent the entire weekend in bed in my hotel room because I was so jaded from a party we had been to the night before. There was the week in Barbados when I didn't go to the beach, sit in the sun or swim in the sea because I was suffering from heroin withdrawal and was too ill to go outside. There was the spa break at Babington House, in Somerset, when I didn't have a single treatment because I was too busy taking cocaine in my room. And then, of course, there was all the money that I had wasted. I'd managed to lose many thousands of pounds as a result of my addiction and had ended up in debt, which I wasn't proud of.

I spent a lot of time during those weeks reflecting on my past relationships and the friends I had made and lost along the way. I was sad about losing Gavin from my life. Even though I was angry with him for the way he had behaved over the paternity test, I couldn't help thinking back to the good times we'd had together: the walks in the park, the early morning breakfasts we had shared, the nights out. There had been a time when Gavin had been my rock, but now he had gone from my life for ever. I'd look at Daisy and see so much of Gavin in her: the way she walked, the way she talked, her height and frame. Though I had resigned myself to the fact that he and I would probably never be friends again, I wished that he would try to form some kind of relationship with Daisy. I wasn't expecting him to play father to her, I just wanted him to appreciate what a wonderful girl she was.

When I looked at my other friendships I found myself questioning how sincere they had really been. John once said to me during a session: 'Put the drugs down and ask yourself how much you really have in common.' That had certainly struck a chord with me. I knew this wasn't true of a lot of the people I was friends with, but it did apply to a few of the group I was hanging out with in London. Now that I had taken myself 'out of the playground' I was starting to see who my friends really were. Living in the country, being pregnant, getting clean, I wasn't exactly the party girl I had once been. A lot of people I knew didn't want to know me any more. One by one they just stopped calling and slipped away from my life, which was something I simply had to accept. I am not going to pretend it didn't hurt me, for it did and I felt deeply wounded by it at times, but I just had to remain philosophical about it. We were living different lives now, we were on separate paths; it was as simple as that.

What frightened me the most during that period was the thought of starting over again, of creating a whole new way of life for myself. In the past when I had got clean I had carried on with business as usual, lived the life of a dry drunk – white knuckling, as they call it in recovery. I had gone to parties, kept up with my group, hung out in my old haunts, but every time I had done it that way I had ended up relapsing. I knew that for my health and sanity I couldn't do that this time, I literally had to physically remove myself from that world. But it was tough. I wondered whether it was possible for me ever to have fun again, whether in my mid-thirties I could make any new friends. I wasn't sure how I would fill my days and nights. Whether it had suited me or not I had always been such a sociable person, and now I spent a great deal of time on my own, and I didn't feel very comfortable about that because I wasn't sure whether I really liked myself any more.

My sessions with John and my NA meetings helped keep me on my path, but I knew it wasn't enough. I needed to feel comfortable in my skin again and feel good about who I was as a person. I knew that only then would I feel truly happy. I had to work on my soul as well as my mind and body, and so I embarked on what I like to see now as a spiritual journey towards my recovery. I went to sessions with a wonderful healer called Suzanne Howlett, whom I had first visited at a retreat called Shambala, in Glastonbury, when I got clean in 2004. During that first session Suzanne had explained to me that people who take drugs open themselves up to negative entities because their abuse creates holes in their auras. That day she worked on me with crystals, and as she laid her hands on my body I felt such a sense of release, as though she had taken a pain away from me that I didn't even know I had. She had told me that day that her guides were saying that I would move to the country and that a beautiful girl spirit wanted to come through to me. I didn't set much store by what she had said at the time, but now that her prophecies had come true I decided to go back and see her. I found my next session with her to be even more rewarding than the first, and I started seeing her on a regular basis. In addition to the healing sessions she would practise reiki healing and reflexology on me.

In an attempt to exorcise my past I went to acupuncture and attended re-birthing sessions. I found re-birthing an incredibly painful exercise, because it meant facing up to my demons, but I knew that the sessions did me a power of good. I saw a lot of Mia, with whom I had formed a close bond. She would come to visit me in the country and we'd sit and talk about life in general for hours at a time. When I felt low or confused, she would make me see sense and encourage me to think positively. I also befriended another healer called Patsy Daniels, who lived locally. As well as the healing sessions she gave me spiritual instruction. She taught me a lot of lessons, the primary one being that to move towards light I would have to go through the dark moments first.

'Why can't I just get there now?' I asked her. 'I'm clean, after all.'

'It's not as simple as that. You can't let go of your old life just like that. You have to let it go in little pieces, bit by bit, otherwise it would be too traumatic for you. You couldn't cope with that. In many ways you are grieving, mourning for your old life, but time will heal that. Eventually, that will pass, you will heal and you will stop revisiting your past and start living in your present,' she told me.

I know that many people regard spiritual healing as a load of self-indulgent mumbo-jumbo, but I am a great believer in it all and I can honestly say that I don't think I would be here today had I not gone on that journey. I needed to come to terms with who I really was before I started using drugs, for there is no question that my addiction blurred my true personality and transformed me into another person. Had I not gone into this process of self re-evaluation I believe that I would have eventually turned to drugs again, and I am not sure I would have survived that this time round.

My spiritual journey was a slow and at times deeply painful one, but I learnt a lot of lessons along the way. Thanks to my network of support I faced my demons head-on. These people equipped me with the tools, strength and knowledge I needed to win my battle against addiction, and I found a sense of peace and serenity. Gradually I got back my sense of purpose and began to feel better about myself. I could see that there was a life outside of drugs, and I wanted to embrace it and live every moment of it to the full.

24

Stepping Out Of The Shadows

When I held Betty for the first time following her birth at the Portland Hospital on 21 November 2005 I knew that there was no turning back. As I cradled this beautiful, blonde, blue-eyed child in my arms I realised just how precious life really was, and I made a promise to myself there and then that I would stay on my path, not just for her sake and for mine, but for Danny's, Daisy's, Alfie's and Frankie's as well. Betty's arrival marked a new era in my life. She had been sent to save me, put on this earth to keep me clean and sober; she was a symbol of hope, a gift I am not sure I really deserved. When the children came to see their new sister later that day, and Danny proudly took her in his arms and introduced her to them, it struck me just how blessed I was. Lying back on my pillows I watched them coo over the latest addition to our family and, despite being tired from the birth, I felt a sense of peace, fulfilment and contentment that I had never experienced before. This is what matters in life, I thought; this is what it is all about. Cherish this moment for ever, for it doesn't get much better than this.

Exciting though it was to be having another child, I have to admit that the run-up to Betty's birth wasn't an easy time for me. There had been days when I felt quite blue and depressed about everything and I wasn't sure whether I was strong enough to get through it. On embarking on my spiritual path I was forced to confront so many negative things about myself that there were moments when I found it difficult to even look at my image in the mirror. Painful as it was, however, I knew that I had to embrace my past if I was ever going to be able to move on and change my life for the better. It wasn't enough just to stop taking drugs, I had to want to stay off them, and to do that I needed to understand just how much damage my use had caused, for only then would I be in a position to appreciate what I had. It wasn't an easy journey for me to take, and I spent a lot of the time during those autumn months in tears, but it was one that paid off. Bit by bit, I began to see the light and understand who I truly was. With the help of my mentors I gradually began to rebuild my life, and by the time Betty was born I felt as though I had, at long last, started to emerge from the shadows.

During that period I had come to see just how selfish I had been over those years. I was forever putting myself first; my wants and desires before everyone else's. I gained a new perspective on life that was less about me and more about others and, armed with the knowledge I had been given, I became determined to put things right and repair some of the damage I had done. I knew, now that I had been given a second chance, that it was time to give something back. I got involved with a charity called Crisis, whose aim was to fight homelessness by giving people the life tools they needed to help them fulfil their potential to transform their lives. What appealed to me about this particular charity was that their mission wasn't just to get people off the streets and give them shelter: what they wanted to do was make sure they never ended up there again, whether it was through taking care of their physical wellbeing, by sending them to doctors or dentists, or through looking after their mental welfare, by re-educating them or giving them counselling. When I learnt that they provided grants for addicts to attend rehabilitation programmes, I knew that I had to get involved. As well as raising funds for Crisis I spent a great deal of time listening to these people's stories, and I began to see just how fortunate I really was. Certainly my addiction had caused me heartache and pain, but I still had a roof over my head, a family who loved me, a handful of friends I could trust and rely on. Most of the people I came into contact with had nothing and no one, save the support of the charity, and yet still they battled on, carried on along their path and looked forward to the future. Their courage and resilience humbled me. 'If they can stay clean with all that they are up against, then I can,' I told Danny after one of my sessions with the charity. 'Next time I feel sorry for myself and am having a moan, I want you to remind me of all that they have been through, and maybe then I will get my problems into some kind of perspective.'

Over that winter my priorities changed. I no longer looked at life and saw it as a void that needed to be punctuated by parties, or filled with drugs. That lifestyle had no meaning for me any more, and I came to understand that it had never made me happy. I had fooled myself into thinking that I was having fun, that the drugs empowered and enlightened me. They had, of course, done nothing of the sort. I had used drugs to mask the pain inside, but in the end all they had done was exacerbate it. My addiction had destroyed so much that was good in my life. It had taken me out of the light, sent me hurtling into the darkness. I knew now that for a time I had been dancing with shadows, and I didn't want to return to that life ever again. I went to parties but never had a good time. I would buy designer clothes to make me feel better and then never wear them. I was friends with people who didn't care about me. I would get a career opportunity and then just waste it. I would take drugs because I believed they made me a better person, but all they did was destroy me. Now that I was clean I could see that it was a meaningless existence, one that brought me nothing but pain.

What brought me happiness now were the simple yet important things in life. Nothing gave me greater joy than being with my family. I loved watching Betty grow and turn from infant into child. I was happy that Alfie and Frankie had settled into their new life in the country, and I was thrilled when Daisy announced that she wanted to spend more time at home. She had fallen completely in love with her little sister, and although she was still based in London whilst she finished school, she would rush back to the country at every opportunity to spend time with us. Danny and I had never been stronger. Now that I was off drugs we no longer argued as we had done before. He said that it was like living with a new person. Even though I had the occasional moment where I got slightly down about life in general, I was no longer crying myself to sleep at night or freaking out when he left to go on tour. If anything I now rather relished the moments when I was alone, for it meant that I had time to myself. I would do things that I had never done in the past like read a book, sketch, go for a walk on my own or sit on the bank of the river and just think. Day by day I grew and learnt to be happy and comfortable in my own company.

In January 2006 I designed my first dress. I was sitting at the kitchen table one afternoon, while the boys were at school and Betty was having her nap, and was idly doodling on my sketchpad when the idea came to me. For some months, since losing my baby weight, I had been looking for something special to wear, but so far without success. There was nothing out there that I liked or felt suited me. I was still running the lace business and had some fabric left over, so I thought I might try to create a dress of my own. I based my design on a vintage dress I had in my wardrobe, which had puffed sleeves and a bow at the front – the only difference would be that my creation would be made from black lace. I showed the drawings to my friend Carol, who was in the house at the time.

'What do you think?'

'It's beautiful, very you. You should get it made up.'

'Really? Are you sure? But I don't even know a dressmaker.'

'I do and she's brilliant,' she said. 'Her name is Parelle, she lives locally and she made my wedding dress, so I can vouch for her.'

Carol was right, Parelle was a brilliant dressmaker. When the sample came back I was completely stunned by the level of her craftsmanship. I had only intended to make a dress for myself, but when friends saw me wearing it and asked where it was from or if I could make one for them I realised that I had an opportunity on my hands. Together with Parelle I started working on some variations on the design, and within a couple of months I had six dresses. I took the samples into

The Cross, a fashionable boutique in Notting Hill Gate which stocked my home accessories, and asked their opinion. With all the designer labels they sold in the store I'd never imagined that they would actually stock my dresses. All I wanted was to get their feedback, so when they told me they would try them out in the store once I had built up my collection I was amazed.

'You know what's strange about all this?' I said to Danny when I came back home that night.

'No. Tell me?'

'All my life I thought that music was my one big passion, the only thing I could ever get excited about, and yet here I am now designing dresses, and in many ways I find it much more satisfying.'

'That doesn't surprise me at all.'

'It doesn't?'

'No, think about it. Both your parents and your grandmother were in the rag trade. It's just as much in your blood as music is. Maybe it is time for a career change.'

It is the spring of 2007 and I am sitting on the edge of the riverbank as I write this final chapter of my story. I have been clean from drugs for over two years now and I consider that to be, aside from my children, one of my greatest achievements. I am not going to pretend that it was a bed of roses, because it hasn't been an easy journey. Although I have never been tempted to stray from my path, there have been times when I have found it hard to keep moving forward. I have struggled with my conscience, beaten myself up about the mistakes I have made, mourned for my past. I have difficult days, the odd sleepless night, and moments when I am filled with despair and remorse, but when it gets like that I just have to stop and take a deep breath and think positively.

My life couldn't be much better than it is right now, and I know that I have a lot to be grateful for. My career is going from strength to strength. The lace business continues to be a success, and my first collection of dresses was launched in October last year at The Cross. They are now stocked at Liberty, and I am starting to receive orders for them from around the world. I know that I have lost friends along the way, but I have also found some new ones, people who I know will keep me on my path and will support me on my journey. My life may not be as rock and roll as it once was, and sometimes I do miss the buzz of that world, but there is also a lot to be said for my new routine. Boring as it might sound to some, I like going to bed early with a good book, I enjoy waking up with the birds and strolling out into the garden with my cup of tea and watching the sun come up. I fill my days with work and I find it hugely satisfying.

Nothing gives me greater pleasure than being with my children, nothing gives me more reward than watching them grow. Betty thrives from day to day. She hurtles through the house at the speed of light and likes to dance and sing. Frankie, who was always behind at school in London, recently came top of his class in a spelling test, which made me very proud, and he is very artistic. Alfie has taken after his father and has just formed his first band, the Little Terrors, in which he plays guitar, and since leaving school Daisy has become a successful model. When she isn't working she spends as much time as she can with us in the country and fills the house with her friends, which I love. She is at an age now where she knows about drugs and we talk about them from time to time. When I recently told her that I had been addicted to heroin she was shocked.

'I just thought you were very sick,' she said. 'There were times, Mum, when I thought you were so ill that I might lose you and that made me very sad.'

'You know what, Daisy, you very nearly did,' was my reply.

And then, of course, there is Danny, the one true love of my life. I know that I have put him through so much over the years, and I am grateful to him for never leaving my side.

When I first started this book I wondered whether I was doing the right thing. I questioned whether I should be telling my tale in the first place, fearing the impact my honesty would have on those around me. But the more I thought about it, the more I realised that I was doing the right thing. I wanted people to see that there is a life outside of drugs, that addiction is a battle that can be won, that you can come out of the darkness into the light; and, more than anything else, I wanted people to see that it is possible to change your life around and have a happy ending.

If you're worried about your own drug use . . .

. . . there are a lot of organisations out there that can help. Some people do go to their GPs as a starting point. Your GP can refer you for specialist treatment. If you feel you can't, you could try Narcotics Anonymous. Their website is great – all the UK meetings are listed so you can find a group in your area, and they have lots of useful resources online.

'NA is a non-profit fellowship or society of men and women for whom drugs had become a major problem. We are recovering addicts who meet regularly to help each other to stay clean. There are no dues or fees. The only requirement for membership is the desire to stop using.'

Contact information:
www.na.org
Helpline: 0845 3733366

There are a number of private clinics that run treatment programmes for addiction of all sorts. Some of the most well known are The Priory, Promis, Clouds and the Charter Nightingale. They are happy to advise about payment plans to cover the costs of treatment.

There is a great NHS drop-in centre in London called The Blenheim Project on Portobello Road that offers support, complementary therapies and counselling. There are also a great many other free, often council- or charity- run services, all over the country. Action on Addiction is a good organisation that can help you to find these.

Contact information:
www.prioryhealthcare.com
www.promis.co.uk
www.clouds.org.uk
www.theblenheimproject.org
www.actiononaddiction.org.uk